HOW TO WRITE CLEARLY

RULES AND EXERCISES ON ENGLISH COMPOSITION

MJP
PUBLISHERS

HOW TO WRITE CLEARLY

RULES AND EXERCISES ON ENGLISH COMPOSITION

Edwin A. Abbott

MJP
PUBLISHERS

Chennai   Trichy   Tirunelveli   New Delhi

MJP
PUBLISHERS

ISBN 978-81-8094-329-4   **MJP Publishers**

All rights reserved   No. 44, Nallathambi Street,

Printed and bound in India   Triplicane, Chennai 600 005

MJP 300   © Publishers, 2019

Publisher :   **C. Janarthanan**

Project Editor :   **C. Ambica**

Publisher's Note

The legacy of a country is in its varied cultural heritage, historical literature, developments in the field of economy and science. The top nations in the world are competing in the field of science, economy and literature. This vast legacy has to be conserved and documented so that it can be bestowed to the future generation. The knowledge of this legacy is slowly getting perished in the present generation due to lack of documentation.

Keeping this in mind, the concern with retrospective acquiring of rare books has been accented recently by the burgeoning reprint industry. MJP Publishers is gratified to retrieve the rare collections with a view to bring back those books that were landmarks in their time.

In this effort, a series of rare books would be republished under the banner, "MJP Publishers". The books in the reprint series have been carefully selected for their contemporary usefulness as well as their historical importance within the intellectual. We reconstruct the book with slight enhancements made for better presentation, without affecting the contents of the original edition.

Most of the works selected for republishing covers a huge range of subjects, from history to anthropology. We believe this reprint edition will be a service to the numerous researchers and practitioners active in this fascinating field. We allow readers to experience the wonder of peering into a scholarly work of the highest order and seminal significance.

MJP Publishers

Preface

Almost every English boy can be taught to write clearly, so far at least as clearness depends upon the arrangement of words. Force, elegance, and variety of style are more difficult to teach, and far more difficult to learn; but clear writing can be reduced to rules. To teach the art of writing clearly is the main object of these Rules and Exercises.

Ambiguity may arise, not only from bad arrangement, but also from other causes—from the misuse of single words, and from confused thought. These causes are not removable by definite rules, and therefore, though not neglected, are not prominently considered in this book. My object rather is to point out some few continually recurring causes of ambiguity, and to suggest definite remedies in each case. Speeches in Parliament, newspaper narratives and articles, and, above all, resolutions at public meetings, furnish abundant instances of obscurity arising from the monotonous neglect of some dozen simple rules.

The art of writing forcibly is, of course, a valuable acquisition—almost as valuable as the art of writing clearly. But forcible expression is not, like clear expression, a mere question of mechanism and of the manipulation of words; it is a much higher power, and implies much more.

Writing clearly does not imply thinking clearly. A man may think and reason as obscurely as Dogberry himself, but he may (though it is not probable that he will) be able to write clearly for all that. Writing clearly—so far as ar-

rangement of words is concerned—is a mere matter of
adverbs, conjunctions, prepositions, and auxiliary verbs,
placed and repeated according to definite rules.[1] Even obscure or illogical thought can be clearly expressed; indeed,
the transparent medium of clear writing is not least beneficial when it reveals the illogical nature of the meaning
beneath it.

On the other hand, if a man is to write forcibly, he
must (to use a well-known illustration) describe Jerusalem
as "sown with salt," not as "captured," and the Jews not
as being "subdued" but as "almost exterminated" by Titus.
But what does this imply? It implies knowledge, and very
often a great deal of knowledge, and it implies also a vivid imagination. The writer must have eyes to see the vivid
side of everything, as well as words to describe what he
sees. Hence forcible writing, and of course tasteful writing
also, is far less a matter of rules than is clear writing; and
hence, though forcible writing is exemplified in the exercises, clear writing occupies most of the space devoted to
the rules.

Boys who are studying Latin and Greek stand in especial need of help to enable them to write a long English
sentence clearly. The periods of Thucydides and Cicero are
not easily rendered into our idiom without some knowledge of the links that connect an English sentence.

There is scarcely any better training, rhetorical as well
as logical, than the task of construing Thucydides into genuine English; but the flat, vague, long-winded Greek-En-
glish and Latin-English imposture that is often tolerated in
our examinations and is allowed to pass current for gen-

---

1. Punctuation is fully discussed in most English Grammars, and is
   therefore referred to in this book only so far as is necessary to point
   out the slovenly fault of trusting too much to punctuation, and too
   little to arrangement.

uine English, diminishes instead of increasing the power that our pupils should possess over their native language. By getting marks at school and college for construing good Greek and Latin into bad English, our pupils systematically unlearn what they may have been allowed to pick up from Milton and from Shakespeare.

I must acknowledge very large obligations to Professor Bain's treatise on "English Composition and Rhetoric," and also to his English Grammar. I have not always been able to agree with Professor Bain as to matters of taste; but I find it difficult to express my admiration for the systematic thoroughness and suggestiveness of his book on Composition. In particular, Professor Bain's rule on the use of "that" and "which" (see Rule 8) deserves to be better known.[2] The ambiguity produced by the confusion between these two forms of the Relative is not a mere fiction of pedants; it is practically serious. Take, for instance, the following sentence, which appeared lately in one of our ablest weekly periodicals: "There are a good many Radical members in the House *who* cannot forgive the Prime Minister for being a Christian." Twenty years hence, who is to say whether the meaning is "*and they*, i.e. *all the Radical*members in the House," or "there are a good many Radical members of the House *that* cannot &c."? Professor Bain, apparently admitting no exceptions to his useful rule, amends many sentences in a manner that seems to me intolerably harsh. Therefore, while laying due stress on the utility of the rule, I have endeavoured to point out and explain the exceptions.

The rules are stated as briefly as possible, and are intended not so much for use by themselves as for reference while the pupil is working at the exercises. Consequently, there is no attempt to prove the rules by accumulations of

2. Before meeting with Professor Bain's rule, I had shown that the difference between the Relatives is generally observed by Shakespeare. See "Shakespearian Grammar," paragraph 259.

examples. The few examples that are given, are given not to prove, but to illustrate the rules. The exercises are intended to be written out and revised, as exercises usually are; but they may also be used for vivâ voce instruction. The books being shut, the pupils, with their written exercises before them, may be questioned as to the reasons for the several alterations they have made. Experienced teachers will not require any explanation of the arrangement or rather non-arrangement of the exercises. They have been purposely mixed together unclassified to prevent the pupil from relying upon anything but his own common sense and industry, to show him what is the fault in each case, and how it is to be amended. Besides references to the rules, notes are attached to each sentence, so that the exercises ought not to present any difficulty to a painstaking boy of twelve or thirteen, provided he has first been fairly trained in English grammar.

The "Continuous Extracts" present rather more difficulty, and are intended for boys somewhat older than those for whom the Exercises are intended. The attempt to modernize, and clarify, so to speak, the style of Burnet, Clarendon, and Bishop Butler,[3] may appear ambitious, and perhaps requires some explanation. My object has, of course, not been to *improve upon* the style of these authors, but to show how their meaning might be expressed more clearly in modern English. The charm of the style is necessarily lost, but if the loss is recognized both by teacher and pupil, there is nothing, in my opinion, to counterbalance the obvious utility of such exercises. Professor Bain speaks to the same effect:[4] "For an English exercise, the matter should in some way or other be supplied, and the pupil disciplined

---

3. Sir Archibald Alison stands on a very different footing. The extracts from this author are intended to exhibit the dangers of verbosity and exaggeration.
4. "English Composition and Rhetoric,"

in giving it expression. I know of no better method than to prescribe passages containing good matter, but in some respects imperfectly worded, to be amended according to the laws and the proprieties of style. Our older writers might be extensively, though not exclusively, drawn upon for this purpose."

To some of the friends whose help has been already acknowledged in "English Lessons for English People," I am indebted for further help in revising these pages. I desire to express especial obligations to the Rev. J. H. Lupton, late Fellow of St. John's College, Cambridge, and Second Master of St. Paul's School, for copious and valuable suggestions; also to several of my colleagues at the City of London School, among whom I must mention in particular the Rev. A. R. Vardy, Fellow of Trinity College, Cambridge.

* * * * *

Before electrotyping the Fourth and Revised Edition, I wish to say one word as to the manner in which this book has been used by my highest class, as a collection of Rules for reference in their construing lessons. In construing, from Thucydides especially, I have found Rules 5, 30, 34, 36, 37, and 40_a_, of great use. The rules about Metaphor and Climax have also been useful in correcting faults of taste in their Latin and Greek compositions. I have hopes that, used in this way, this little book may be of service to the highest as well as to the middle classes of our schools.

Contents

INDEX OF RULES

I CLEARNESS AND FORCE

Words

1. Use words in their proper sense.

2. Avoid exaggerations.

3. Avoid useless circumlocution and "fine writing."

4. Be careful in the use of "not ... and," "any," "but," "only," "not ... or," "that."

4*a*. Be careful in the use of ambiguous words, *e.g.* "certain."

5. Be careful in the use of "he," "it," "they," "these," &c.

6. Report a speech in the First Person, where necessary to avoid ambiguity.

6*a*. Use the Third Person where the exact words of the speaker are not intended to be given.

6*b*. Omission of "that" in a speech in the Third Person.

7. When you use a Participle implying "when," "while," "though," or "that," show clearly by the context what is implied.

8. When using the Relative Pronoun, use "who" or "which," if the meaning is "and he" or "and it," "for

he" or "for it." In other cases use "that," if euphony allows. Exceptions.

9.   Do not use "and which" for "which."

10.   Equivalents for the Relative: (*a*) Participle or Adjective; (*b*) Infinitive; (*c*) "Whereby," "whereto," &c.; (*d*) "If a man;" (*e*) "And he," "and this," &c.; (*f*) "what;" (*g*) omission of Relative.

10*a'*. Repeat the Antecedent before the Relative, where the non-repetition causes any ambiguity.

11.   Use particular for general terms. Avoid abstract Nouns.

11*a*. Avoid Verbal Nouns where Verbs can be used.

12.   Use particular persons instead of a class.

13.   Use metaphor instead of literal statement.

14.   Do not confuse metaphor.

14*a*. Do not mix metaphor with literal statement.

14*b*. Do not use poetic metaphor to illustrate a prosaic subject.

ORDER OF WORDS IN A SENTENCE

15.   Emphatic words must stand in emphatic positions; *i.e.*, for the most part, at the beginning or the end of the sentence.

15*a*. Unemphatic words must, as a rule, be kept from the end. Exceptions.

15*b*. An interrogation sometimes gives emphasis.

16.   The Subject, if unusually emphatic, should often be transferred from the beginning of the sentence.

17. The Object is sometimes placed before the Verb for emphasis.

18. Where several words are emphatic, make it clear which is the most emphatic. Emphasis can sometimes be given by adding an epithet, or an intensifying word.

19. Words should be as near as possible to the words with which they are grammatically connected.

20. Adverbs should be placed next to the words they are intended to qualify.

21. "Only"; the strict rule is that "only" should be placed before the word it affects.

22. When "not only" precedes "but also," see that each is followed by the same part of speech.

23. "At least," "always," and other adverbial adjuncts, sometimes produce ambiguity.

24. Nouns should be placed near the Nouns that they define.

25. Pronouns should follow the Nouns to which they refer, without the intervention of any other Noun.

26. Clauses that are grammatically connected should be kept as close together as possible. Avoid parentheses.

27. In conditional sentences, the antecedent or "if-clauses" must be kept distinct from the consequent clauses.

28. Dependent clauses preceded by "that" should be kept distinct from those that are independent.

29. Where there are several infinitives, those that are dependent on the same word must be kept distinct from those that are not.

30.   The principle of Suspense.

30*a*.   It is a violation of the principle of suspense to in-
         troduce unexpectedly at the end of a long sentence,
         some short and unemphatic clause beginning with
         (*a*) "not," (*b*) "which."

31.   Suspense must not be excessive.

32.   In a sentence with "if," "when," "though," &c., put the
       "if-clause," antecedent, or protasis, first.

33.   Suspense is gained by placing a Participle or Adjec-
       tive, that qualifies the Subject, before the Subject.

34.   Suspensive Conjunctions, *e.g.* "either," "not only," "on
       the one hand," &c., add clearness.

35.   Repeat the Subject, where its omission would cause
       obscurity or ambiguity.

36.   Repeat a Preposition after an intervening Conjunc-
       tion, especially if a Verb and an Object also inter-
       vene.

37.   Repeat Conjunctions, Auxiliary Verbs, and Pronom-
       inal Adjectives.

37*a*.   Repeat Verbs after the Conjunctions "than," "as," &c.

38.   Repeat the Subject, or some other emphatic word, or
       a summary of what has been said, if the sentence is
       so long that it is difficult to keep the thread of mean-
       ing unbroken.

39.   Clearness is increased, when the beginning of the
       sentence prepares the way for the middle, and the
       middle for the end, the whole forming a kind of as-
       cent. This ascent is called "climax."

40.   When the thought is expected to ascend, but de-
       scends, feebleness, and sometimes confusion, is the
       result. The descent is called "bathos."

40*a.* A new construction should not be introduced unexpectedly.

41. Antithesis adds force and often clearness.

42. Epigram.

43. Let each sentence have one, and only one, principal subject of thought. Avoid heterogeneous sentences.

44. The connection between different sentences must be kept up by Adverbs used as Conjunctions, or by means of some other connecting words at the beginning of the sentence.

45. The connection between two long sentences or paragraphs sometimes requires a short intervening sentence showing the transition of thought.

II BREVITY

46. Metaphor is briefer than literal statement.

47. General terms are briefer, though less forcible, than particular terms.

47*a.* A phrase may sometimes be expressed by a word.

48. Participles may often be used as brief (though sometimes ambiguous) equivalents of phrases containing Conjunctions and Verbs.

49. Participles, Adjectives, Participial Adjectives, and Nouns may be used as equivalents for phrases containing the Relative.

50. A statement may sometimes be briefly implied instead of being expressed at length.

51. Conjunctions may be omitted. Adverbs, *e.g.* "very," "so." Exaggerated epithets, *e.g.* "incalculable," "unprecedented."

51*a.* The imperative may be used for "if &c."

52. Apposition may be used, so as to convert two sentences into one.

53. Condensation may be effected by not repeating (1) the common Subject of several Verbs; (2) the common Object of several Verbs or Prepositions.

54. Tautology. Repeating what may be implied.

55. Parenthesis maybe used with advantage to brevity.

56. Brevity often clashes with clearness. Let clearness be the first consideration.

CLEARNESS AND FORCE

Numbers in brackets refer to the Rules

WORDS

1. Use words in their proper sense.

Write, not "His apparent guilt justified his friends in disowning him," but "his evident guilt." "Conscious" and "aware," "unnatural" and "supernatural," "transpire" and "occur," "circumstance" and "event," "reverse" and "converse," "eliminate" and "elicit," are often confused together.

This rule forbids the use of the same word in different senses. "It is in my *power* to refuse your request, and since I have *power* to do this, I may lawfully do it." Here the second "power" is used for "authority."

This rule also forbids the slovenly use of "nice," "awfully," "delicious," "glorious," & c.

2. Avoid exaggerations.

"The boundless plains in the heart of the empire furnished inexhaustible supplies of corn, that would have almost sufficed for twice the population."

Here "inexhaustible" is inconsistent with what follows. The words "unprecedented," "incalculable," "very," and "stupendous" are often used in the same loose way.

3. Avoid useless circumlocution and "fine writing."

"Her Majesty here partook of lunch." Write "lunched."

"Partook of" implies sharing, and is incorrect as well as lengthy.

So, do not use "apex" for "top," "species" for "kind," "individual" for "man," "assist" for "help," &c.

4. Be careful how you use the following words: "not ... and," "any," "only," "not ... or," "that."[5]

And. See below, "Or."

Any—"I am not bound to receive any messenger that you send." Does this mean every, or a single? Use "every" or "a single."

Not—(1) "I do not intend to help you, because you are my enemy &c." ought to mean (2), "I intend not to help you, and my reason for not helping you is, because you are my enemy." But it is often wrongly used to mean (3), "I intend to help you, not because you are my enemy (but because you are poor, blind, &c.)." In the latter case, not ought to be separated from intend. By distinctly marking the limits to which the influence of not extends, the ambiguity may be removed.

Only—is often used ambiguously for alone. "The rest help me to revenge myself; you only advise me to wait." This ought to mean, "you only advise, instead of helping;" but in similar sentences "you only" is often used for "you alone."

Or—When "or" is preceded by a negative, as "I do not want butter *or* honey," "or" ought not, strictly speaking, to

---

5. *For,* at the beginning of a sentence, sometimes causes temporary doubt, while the reader is finding out whether it is used as a conjunction or preposition.

be used like "and," nor like "nor." The strict use of "not ... or" would be as follows:—

"You say you don't want both butter *and* honey—you want butter *or* honey; I, on the contrary, *do not want butter or honey*—I want them both."

Practically, however, this meaning is so rare, that "I don't want butter or honey" is regularly used for "I want neither butter nor honey." But where there is the slightest danger of ambiguity, it is desirable to use nor.

The same ambiguity attends "not ... and." "I do not see Thomas *and* John" is commonly used for "I see neither Thomas nor John;" but it might mean, "I do not see them both—I see only one of them."

That—The different uses of "that" produce much ambiguity, *e.g.* "I am so much surprised by this statement *that* I am desirous of resigning, *that* I scarcely know what reply to make." Here it is impossible to tell, till one has read past "resigning," whether the first "that" depends upon "so" or "statement." Write: "The statement that I am desirous of resigning surprises me so much that I scarcely know &c."

4a.　Be careful in the use of ambiguous words, e.g. "certain."

"Certain" is often used for "some," as in "Independently of his earnings, he has a certain property," where the meaning might be "unfailing."

Under this head may be mentioned the double use of words, such as "left" in the same form and sound, but different in meaning. Even where there is no obscurity, the juxtaposition of the same word twice used in two senses is inelegant, *e.g.* (Bain), "He turned to the *left* and *left* the room."

I have known the following slovenly sentence misunderstood: "Our object is that, with the aid of practice, we may sometime arrive at the point where we think eloquence in its most praiseworthy form *to lie*." "To lie" has been supposed to mean "to deceive."

5. Be careful how you use "he," "it," "they," "these," & c. or "which". The ambiguity arising from the use of he applying to different persons is well known.

"He told his friend that if he did not feel better in half an hour he thought he had better return.".

Much ambiguity is also caused by excessive use of such phrases as *in this way, of this sort,* & c.

"God, foreseeing the disorders of human nature, has given us certain passions and affections which arise from, or whose objects are, these disorders. *Of this sort* are fear, resentment, compassion."

Repeat the noun: "Among these passions and affections are fear &c."

Two distinct uses of *it* may be noted. *It,* when referring to something that precedes, may be called "retrospective;" but when to something that follows, "prospective." In "Avoid indiscriminate charity: *it* is a crime," "it" is retrospective.[6] In "*It* is a crime to give indiscriminately," "it" is prospective.

The prospective "it," if productive of ambiguity, can often be omitted by using the infinitive as a subject: "To give indiscriminately is a crime."

6. **Report a speech in the First, not the Third Person, where necessary to avoid ambiguity.** Speeches in the third person afford a particular, though very com-

6. *It* should refer (1) either to the Noun immediately preceding, or to some Noun superior to all intervening Nouns in emphasis.

mon case, of the general ambiguity mentioned in (5). Instead of "He told his friend that if *he* did not feel better &c.," write "He said to his friend, 'If, *I* (or *you*) don't feel better &c.'"

6a. Sometimes, where the writer cannot know the exact words, or where the exact words are unimportant, or lengthy and uninteresting, the Third Person is pref- erable. Thus, where Essex is asking Sir Robert Cecil that Francis Bacon may be appointed Attorney-Gen- eral, the dialogue is (as it almost always is in Lord Macaulay's writings) in the First Person, *except where it becomes tedious and uninteresting so as to require condensation*, and then it drops into the Third Person:

"Sir Robert *had nothing to say but* that he thought his own abilities equal to the place which he hoped to obtain, and that his father's long services deserved such a mark of gratitude from the Queen."

6b. **Omission of "that" in a speech reported in the Third Person**—Even when a speech is reported in the third person, "that" need not always be inserted before the dependent verb. Thus, instead of "He said that he took it ill that his promises were not believed," we may write, "'He took it ill,' he said, 'that &c.'" This gives a little more life, and sometimes more clearness also.

7. When you use a Participle, as "walking," implying "when," "while," "though," "that," make it clear by the context what is implied.

"Republics, in the first instance, are never desired for their own sakes. I do not think they will finally be desired at all, *unaccompanied* by courtly graces and good breeding."

Here there is a little doubt whether the meaning is "*since* they are, or, *if* they are, unaccompanied."

That or when—"Men *walking* (*that* walk, or *when* they walk) on ice sometimes fall."

It is better to use "men walking" to mean "men *when* they walk." If the relative is meant, use "men that walk," instead of the participle.

(1) "*While* he was } *Walking* on { (1) the road, } he fell."

(2) "*Because* he was } { (2) the ice, }

When the participle precedes the subject, it generally implies a cause: "*Seeing* this, he retired." Otherwise it generally has its proper participial meaning, *e.g.* "He retired, *keeping* his face towards us." If there is any ambiguity, write "*on* seeing,"—"*at the same time,* or *while,* keeping."

(1) "*Though* he was} {(1) he nevertheless stood} { his ground."

(2) "*Since* he was } *Struck* with terror, {(2) he rapidly retreated."

(3) "*If* he is } {(3) he will soon retreat."

8. When using the Relative Pronoun, use "who" and "which" where the meaning is "and he, it, &c.," "for he, it, &c." In other cases use "that," if euphony allows.

"I heard this from the inspector, *who* (and he) heard it from the guard *that* travelled with the train."

"Fetch me (all) the books *that* lie on the table, and also the pamphlets, *which* (and these) you will find on the floor."

An adherence to this rule would remove much ambiguity. Thus: "There was a public-house next door, *which* was a great nuisance," means "*and this* (*i.e.* the fact of its being next door) was a great nuisance;" whereas *that* would have meant "Next door was a public-house *that* (*i.e.* the public-house) was a great nuisance." "Who," "which," &c. introduce a new fact about the antecedent, whereas "that" introduces something without which the antecedent is incomplete or undefined.* Thus, in the first example above, "inspector" is complete in itself, and "who" introduces a new *fact* about him; "guard" is incomplete, and requires "*that* travelled with the train" to complete the meaning.

It is not, and cannot be, maintained that this rule, though observed in Elizabethan English, is observed by our best modern authors. (Probably a general impression that "that" cannot be used to refer to persons has assisted "who" in supplanting "that" as a relative.) But the convenience of the rule is so great that beginners in composition may with advantage adhere to the rule. The following are some of the cases where *who* and *which* are mostly used, contrary to the rule, instead of *that*.

Exceptions

(*a*) When the antecedent is defined, *e.g.* by a possessive case, modern English uses *who* instead of *that*. It is rare, though it would be useful,[7] to say "His English friends *that* had not seen him" for "the English friends, or those of his English friends, that had not seen him."

(*b*) *That* sounds ill when separated from its verb and from its antecedents, and emphasized by isolation: "There are many persons *that*, though unscrupulous, are commonly good-tempered, and *that*, if not strongly incited by self-interest, are ready for the most part to think of the interest of their neighbours."

---

7. So useful that, on mature consideration, I am disposed to adopt "that" here and in several of the following exceptional cases.

Shakespeare frequently uses *who* after *that* when the relative is repeated. See "Shakespearian Grammar,".

(*c*)   If the antecedent is qualified by *that*, the relative must not be *that*. Besides other considerations, the repetition is disagreeable. Addison ridicules such language as "*That* remark *that* I made yesterday is not *that that* I said *that* I regretted *that* I had made."

(*d*)   *That* cannot be preceded by a preposition, and hence throws the preposition to the end. "This is the rule *that* I adhere *to*." This is perfectly good English, though sometimes unnecessarily avoided. But, with some prepositions, the construction is harsh and objectionable, *e.g.* "This is the mark *that* I jumped *beyond*," "Such were the prejudices *that* he rose *above*." The reason is that some of these disyllabic prepositions are used as adverbs, and, when separated from their nouns, give one the impression that they are used as adverbs.

(*e*)   After pronominal adjectives used for personal pronouns, modern English prefers *who*. "There are many, others, several, those, *who* can testify &c."

(*f*)   After *that* used as a conjunction there is sometimes a dislike to use *that* as a relative.

9.   **Do not use redundant "and" before "which."**[8]

"I gave him a very interesting book for a present, *and which* cost me five shillings."

In short sentences the absurdity is evident, but in long sentences it is less evident, and very common.

"A petition was presented for rescinding that portion of the bye-laws which permits application of public money to support sectarian schools over which ratepayers have no

8.   Of course "and which" may be used where "which" precedes.

control, this being a violation of the principle of civil and religious liberty, *and which* the memorialists believe would provoke a determined and conscientious resistance."

Here *which* ought grammatically to refer to "portion" or "schools." But it seems intended to refer to "violation." Omit "and," or repeat "a violation" before "which," or turn the sentence otherwise.

10. **Equivalents for Relative**

(a)   **Participle**—"Men *thirsting* (for 'men *that thirst*') for revenge are not indifferent to plunder." The objection to the participle is that here, as often, it creates a little ambiguity. The above sentence may mean, "men, *when* they thirst," or "*though* they thirst," as well as "men *that* thirst." Often however there is no ambiguity: "I have documents *proving* this conclusively."

(b)   **Infinitive**—Instead of "He was the first *that* entered" you can write "*to* enter;" for "He is not a man *who* will act dishonestly," "*to* act." This equivalent cannot often be used.

(c)   **Whereby, wherein**, &c., can sometimes be used for "by *which*," "in *which*," so as to avoid a harsh repetition of "*which*." "The means *whereby* this may be effected." But this use is somewhat antiquated.

(d)   **If**—"The man *that* does not care for music is to be pitied" can be written (though not so forcibly), "*If* a man does not care for music, he is to be pitied." It is in long sentences that this equivalent will be found most useful.

(e)   **And this**—"He did his best, *which* was all that could be expected," can be written, "*and this* was all that, &c."

(*f*) **What**—"Let me repeat *that which*[9] you ought to know, that *that which* is worth doing is worth doing well." "Let me repeat, *what* you ought to know, that *what* is worth doing is worth doing well."

(*g*) **Omission of Relative**—It is sometimes thought ungrammatical to omit the relative, as in "The man (that) you speak of." On the contrary, *that* when an object (not when a subject) may be omitted, wherever the antecedent and the subject of the relative sentence are brought into juxtaposition by the omission.

10a. **Repeat the Antecedent in some new form, where there is any ambiguity.** This is particularly useful after a negative: "He said that he would not even hear me, *which* I confess I had expected." Here the meaning may be, "I had expected that he would," or "that he would not, hear me." Write, "*a refusal*, or, *a favour*, that I confess I had expected."

11. **Use particular for general terms**—This is a most important rule. Instead of "I have neither the necessaries of life nor the means of procuring them," write (if you can *with truth*), "I have not a crust of bread, nor a penny to buy one."

CAUTION—There is a danger in this use. The meaning is vividly expressed but sometimes may be exaggerated or imperfect. Crust of bread may be an exaggeration; on the other hand, if the speaker is destitute not only of bread, but also of shelter and clothing, then crust of bread is an imperfect expression of the meaning.

---

9. "That which," where *that* is an *object*, e.g. "then (set forth) *that which* is worse," *St. John* ii. 10, is rare in modern English

In philosophy and science, where the language ought very often to be inclusive and brief, general and not particular terms must be used.

11a. **Avoid Verbal Nouns where Verbs can be used instead.** The disadvantage of the use of Verbal Nouns is this, that, unless they are immediately preceded by prepositions, they are sometimes liable to be confounded with participles. The following is an instance of an excessive use of Verbal Nouns:

"The pretended confession of the secretary was only collusion to lay the jealousies of the king's *favouring* popery, which still hung upon him, notwithstanding his *writing* on the Revelation, and *affecting* to enter on all occasions into controversy, *asserting* in particular that the Pope was Antichrist."

Write "notwithstanding that he wrote and affected &c."

12. **Use a particular Person instead of a class.**

"What is the splendour of *the greatest monarch* compared with the beauty of *a flower?*" "What is the splendour of Solomon compared with the beauty of a daisy?"

Under this head may come the forcible use of Noun for Adjective: "This fortress is *weakness* itself."

An excess of this use is lengthy and pedantically bombastic, *e.g.*, the following paraphrase for "in every British colony:"—"under Indian palm-groves, amid Australian gum-trees, in the shadow of African mimosas, and beneath Canadian pines."

13. **Use Metaphor instead of literal statement.**

"The ship *ploughs* the sea" is clearer than "the ship *cleaves* the sea," and shorter than "the ship *cleaves* the sea *as a plough cleaves the land.*"

Of course there are some subjects for which Metaphor should not be used.

14. Do not confuse Metaphor.

"In a moment the thunderbolt was upon them, *deluging* their country with invaders."

The following is attributed to Sir Boyle Roche: "Mr. Speaker, I smell a rat, I see him brewing in the air; but, mark me, I shall yet nip him in the bud."

Some words, once metaphorical, have ceased to be so regarded. Hence many good writers say "*under* these *circumstances*" instead of "*in* these circumstances."

An excessive regard for disused metaphor savours of pedantry: disregard is inelegant. Write, not, "*unparalleled* complications," but "*unprecedented* complications;" and "*he threw light on* obscurities," instead of "*he unravelled* obscurities."

14a. Do not introduce literal statement immediately after Metaphor.

"He was the father of Chemistry, and brother to the Earl of Cork."

"He was a very thunderbolt of war,
And was lieutenant to the Earl of Mar."

14b. **Do not use poetic metaphor to illustrate a prosaic subject.** Thus, we may say "a poet *soars*," or even, though rarely, "a nation *soars* to greatness," but you could not say "Consols *soared to* 94-1/2." Even commonplace subjects may be illustrated by metaphor: for it is a metaphor, and quite unobjectionable, to say "Consols *mounted,* or *jumped* to 94-1/2." But commonplace subjects must be illustrated by metaphor that is commonplace.

ORDER OF WORDS IN A SENTENCE

15. **Emphatic words must stand in emphatic positions; i.e. for the most part, at the beginning or at the end of the sentence.** This rule occasionally supersedes the common rules about position. Thus, the place for an adverb, as a rule, should be between the subject and verb: "He *quickly* left the room;" but if *quickly* is to be emphatic, it must come at the beginning or end, as in "I told him to leave the room slowly, but he left *quickly*."

Adjectives, in clauses beginning with "if" and "though," often come at the beginning for emphasis: "*Insolent* though he was, he was silenced at last."

15a. **Unemphatic words must, as a rule, be kept from the end of the sentence.** It is a common fault to break this rule by placing a short and unemphatic predicate at the end of a long sentence.

"To know some Latin, even if it be nothing but a few Latin roots, *is useful.*" Write, "It is useful, &c."

So "the evidence proves how kind to his inferiors *he is.*"

Often, where an adjective or auxiliary verb comes at the end, the addition of an emphatic adverb justifies the position, *e.g.* above, "is *very* useful," "he has *invariably* been."

A short "chippy" ending, even though emphatic, is to be avoided. It is abrupt and unrhythmical, *e.g.* "The soldier, transfixed with the spear, *writhed.*" We want a *longer* ending, "fell writhing to the ground," or, "writhed in the agonies of death." A "chippy" ending is common in bad construing from Virgil.

Exceptions

Prepositions and pronouns attached to emphatic words need not be moved from the end; e.g. "He does no harm that I hear of." "Bear witness how I loved him."

N.B. In all styles, especially in letter-writing, a final emphasis must not be so frequent as to become obtrusive and monotonous.

15b. **An interrogation sometimes gives emphasis.** "No one can doubt that the prisoner, had he been really guilty, would have shown some signs of remorse," is not so emphatic as "Who can doubt, Is it possible to doubt, &c.?"

Contrast "No one ever names Wentworth without thinking of &c." with "But Wentworth,—who ever names him without thinking of those harsh dark features, ennobled by their expression into more than the majesty of an antique Jupiter?"

16. **The subject, if unusually emphatic, should often be removed from the beginning of the sentence.** The beginning of the sentence is an emphatic position, though mostly not so emphatic as the end. Therefore the principal subject of a sentence, being emphatic, and being wanted early in the sentence to tell us what the sentence is about, comes as a rule, at or near the beginning: "*Thomas* built this house."

Hence, since the beginning is the *usual* place for the subject, if we want to emphasize "Thomas" *unusually*, we must remove "Thomas" from the beginning: "This house was built by *Thomas*," or "It was *Thomas* that built this house."

Thus, the emphasis on "conqueror" is not quite so strong in "*A mere conqueror* ought not to obtain from us the reverence that is due to the great benefactors of mankind," as in "We ought not to bestow the reverence that is due to the great benefactors of mankind, *upon a mere conqueror.*" Considerable, but less emphasis and greater smoothness (19) will be obtained by writing the sentence thus: "We ought not to bestow upon a mere conqueror &c."

Where the same subject stands first in several consecutive sentences, it rises in emphasis, and need not be removed from the beginning, even though unusual emphasis be required:

"The captain was the life and soul of the expedition. *He* first pointed out the possibility of advancing; *he* warned them of the approaching scarcity of provisions; *he* showed how they might replenish their exhausted stock &c."

17. **The object is sometimes placed before the verb for emphasis.** This is most common in antithesis. "*Jesus* I know, and *Paul* I know; but who are ye?" "*Some* he imprisoned, *others* he put to death."

Even where there is no antithesis the inversion is not uncommon:

"Military *courage*, the boast of the sottish German, of the frivolous and prating Frenchman, of the romantic and arrogant Spaniard, he neither possesses nor values."

This inversion sometimes creates ambiguity in poetry, *e.g.* "The son the father slew," and must be sparingly used in prose.

Sometimes the position of a word may be considered appropriate by some, and inappropriate by others, according to different interpretations of the sentence. Take as an example, "Early in the morning the nobles and gentlemen who attended on the king assembled in the great hall of the castle; and here they began to talk of what a dreadful storm it had been the night before. But Macbeth could scarcely understand what they said, for he was thinking of something worse." The last sentence has been amended by Professor Bain into "*What they said*, Macbeth could scarcely understand." But there appears to be an antithesis between the guiltless nobles who can think about the weather, and the guilty Macbeth who cannot. Hence, "what they said" ought not, and "Macbeth" ought, to be emphasized: and therefore "Macbeth" ought to be retained at the beginning of the sentence.

The same author alters, "The praise of judgment Virgil has justly contested with him, but his invention remains yet unrivalled," into "Virgil has justly contested with him the praise of judgment, but no one has yet rivalled his invention"—an alteration which does not seem to emphasize sufficiently the antithesis between what had been 'contested,' on the one hand, and what remained as yet 'unrivalled' on the other.

More judiciously Professor Bain alters, "He that tells a lie is not sensible how great a task he undertakes; for he must be forced to invent twenty more to maintain one," into "for, to maintain one, he must invent twenty more," putting the emphatic words in their emphatic place, at the end.

18. **Where several words are emphatic, make it clear which is the most emphatic.** Thus, in "The state was made, under the pretence of serving it, in reality the prize of their contention to each of these opposite parties," it is unpleasantly doubtful whether the writer means (1) *state* or (2) *parties* to be emphatic.

If (1), "As for the *state*, these two parties, under the pretence of serving it, converted it into a prize for their contention." If (2), write, "Though served in profession, the state was in reality converted into a prize for their contention by these two *parties*." In (1) *parties* is subordinated, in (2) *state*.

Sometimes the addition of some intensifying word serves to emphasize. Thus, instead of "To effect this they used all devices," we can write "To effect this they used *every conceivable device*." So, if we want to emphasize fidelity in "The business will task your skill and fidelity," we can write "Not only your skill *but also* your fidelity." This, however, sometimes leads to exaggerations.

Sometimes antithesis gives emphasis, as in "You *do* not know this, but you *shall* know it." Where antithesis cannot be used, the emphasis must be expressed by turning the sentence, as "I *will make you* know it," or by some addition, as "You shall *hereafter* know it."

19. **Words should be as near as possible to the words with which they are grammatically connected.**

20. **Adverbs should be placed next to the words they are intended to affect.** When unemphatic, adverbs come between the subject and the verb, or, if the tense is compound, between the parts of the compound tense: "He *quickly* left the room;" "He has *quickly* left the room;" but, when emphatic, after the verb: "He left, or has left, the room *quickly*."[10] When such a sentence as the latter is followed by a present participle, there arises ambiguity. "I told him to go slowly, but he left the room *quickly*, dropping the purse on the floor." Does *quickly* here modify *left* or *dropping*? The

---

10. Sometimes the emphatic Adverb comes at the beginning, and causes the transposition of an Auxiliary Verb, "*Gladly* do I consent."

remedy[11] is, to give the adverb its unemphatic place, "He *quickly* left the room, dropping &c.," or else to avoid the participle, thus: "He *quickly* dropped the purse and left the room," or "He dropped the purse and *quickly* left the room."

21. "Only" requires careful use. The strict[12] rule is, that "only" should be placed before the word affected by it.

The following is ambiguous:

"The heavens are not open to the faithful *only* at intervals."

The best rule is to avoid placing "only" between two emphatic words, and to avoid using "only" where "alone" can be used instead.

In strictness perhaps the three following sentences:

(1)   He *only* beat three,

(2)   He beat *only* three,

(3)   He beat three *only*, ought to be explained, severally, thus:

(1)   He did no more than beat, did not kill, three.

(2)   He beat no more than three.

(3)   He beat three, and that was all he did. (Here *only* modifies the whole of the sentence and depreciates the action.)

But the best authors sometimes transpose the word. "He *only* lived" ought to mean "he did not die or make any great sacrifice;" but "He *only* lived but till he was a man"

---

11. Of course punctuation will remove the ambiguity; but it is better to express oneself clearly, as far as possible, independently of punctuation

12. Professor Bain

(*Macbeth*, v. 8. 40) means "He lived *only* till he was a man." Compare also, "Who *only* hath immortality."

Only at the beginning of a statement = but. "I don't like to importune you, only I know you'll forgive me." Before an imperative it diminishes the favour asked: "Only listen to me." This use of only is mostly confined to letters.

Very often, *only* at the beginning of a sentence is used for *alone*: "*Only* ten came," "*Only* Cœsar approved." *Alone* is less ambiguous. The ambiguity of *only* is illustrated by such a sentence as, "Don't hesitate to bring a few friends of yours to shoot on my estate at any time. *Only* five (fifteen) came yesterday," which might mean, "I don't mind a *few*, *only* don't bring so many as *fifteen*;" or else "Don't hesitate to bring a few *more*; no more than *five* came yesterday." In conversation, ambiguity is prevented by emphasis; but in a letter, *only* thus used might cause unfortunate mistakes. Write "Yesterday *only* five came," if you mean "no more than five."

22. **When "not only" precedes "but also," see that each is followed by the same part of speech.**

"He *not only* gave me advice *but also* help" is wrong. Write "He gave me, *not only* advice, *but also* help." On the other hand, "He *not only* gave me a grammar, *but also* lent me a dictionary," is right. Take an instance. "He spoke *not only* forcibly *but also* tastefully (adverbs), and this too, *not only* before a small audience, *but also* in (prepositions) a large public meeting, and his speeches were *not only* successful, *but also* (adjective) worthy of success."

23. **"At least," "always," and other adverbial adjuncts, sometimes produce ambiguity.**

"I think you will find my Latin exercise, *at all events*, as good as my cousin's." Does this mean (1) "my Latin exercise, though not perhaps my other exercises;" or (2), "Though not very good, yet, at all events, as good as my cousin's"? Write for (1), "My Latin exercise, at all events, you will find &c." and for (2), "I think you will find my Latin exercise as good as my cousin's, at all events."

The remedy is to avoid placing "at all events" between two emphatic words.

As an example of the misplacing of an adverbial adjunct, take "From abroad he received most favourable reports, but in the City he heard that a panic had broken out on the Exchange, and that the funds were fast falling." This ought to mean that the "hearing," and not (as is intended) that the "breaking out of the panic," took place in the City.

In practice, an adverb is often used to qualify a remote word, where the latter is *more emphatic than any nearer word*. This is very common when the Adverbial Adjunct is placed in an emphatic position at the beginning of the sentence: "*On this very spot* our guide declared that Claverhouse had fallen."

24.   **Nouns should be placed near the nouns that they define.** In the very common sentence "The death is announced of Mr. John Smith, an author whose works &c.," the transposition is probably made from a feeling that, if we write "The death of Mr. John Smith is announced," we shall be obliged to begin a new sentence, "He was an author whose works &c." But the difficulty can be removed by writing "We regret to announce, or, we are informed of, the death of Mr. John Smith, an author, &c."

25.   **Pronouns should follow the nouns to which they refer without the intervention of another noun.** Avoid, "John Smith, the son of Thomas Smith, *who* gave me this book," unless *Thomas Smith* is the anteced-

ent of *who.* Avoid also "John supplied Thomas with money: *he* (John) was very well off."

When, however, one of two preceding nouns is decidedly superior to the other in emphasis, the more emphatic may be presumed to be the noun referred to by the pronoun, even though the noun of inferior emphasis intervenes. Thus: "At this moment the colonel came up, and took the place of the wounded general. *He* gave orders to halt." Here *he* would naturally refer to *colonel,* though *general* intervenes. A *conjunction* will often show that a pronoun refers to the subject of the preceding sentence, and not to another intervening noun. "The sentinel at once took aim at the approaching soldier, and fired. He *then* retreated to give the alarm."

It is better to adhere, in most cases, to Rule 25, which may be called (Bain) the Rule of Proximity. The Rule of Emphasis, of which an instance was given in the last paragraph, is sometimes misleading. A distinction might be drawn by punctuating thus:

"David the father of Solomon, who slew Goliath." "David, the father of Solomon who built the Temple." But the propriety of omitting a comma in each case is questionable, and it is better to write so as not to be at the mercy of commas.

26. **Clauses that are grammatically connected should be kept as close together as possible.** The introduction of parentheses violating this rule often produced serious ambiguity. Thus, in the following: "The result of these observations appears to be in opposition to the view now generally received in this country, that in muscular effort the substance of the muscle itself undergoes disintegration." Here it is difficult to tell whether the theory of "disintegration" is (1) "the re-

sult," or, as the absence of a comma after "be" would indicate, (2) "in opposition to the result of these observations." If (1) is intended, add "and to prove" after "country;" if (2), insert "which is" after "country."

There is an excessive complication in the following:—"It cannot, at all events, if the consideration demanded by a subject of such importance from any one professing to be a philosopher, be given, be denied that &c."

Where a speaker feels that his hearers have forgotten the connection of the beginning of the sentence, he should repeat what he has said; *e.g.* after the long parenthesis in the last sentence he should recommence, "it cannot, I say, be denied." In writing, however, this licence must be sparingly used.

A short parenthesis, or modifying clause, will not interfere with clearness, especially if antithesis he used, so as to show the connection between the different parts of the sentence, *e.g.* "A modern newspaper statement, *though probably true*, would be laughed at if quoted in a book as testimony; but the letter of a court gossip is thought good historical evidence if written some centuries ago." Here, to place "though probably true" at the beginning of the sentence would not add clearness, and would impair the emphasis of the contrast between "a modern newspaper statement" and "the letter of a court gossip."

27.   In conditional sentences, the antecedent clauses must be kept distinct from the consequent clauses.There is ambiguity in "The lesson intended to be taught by these manoeuvres will be lost, if the plan of operations is laid down too definitely beforehand, and the affair degenerates into a mere review." Begin, in any case, with the antecedent, "If the plan," &c. Next write, according to the meaning: (1) "If the

plan is laid down, and the affair degenerates &c., then the lesson will be lost;" or (2) " ... then the lesson ... will be lost, and the affair degenerates into a mere review."

28. **Dependent clauses preceded by "that" should be kept distinct from those that are independent.**

Take as an example:

(1) "He replied that he wished to help them, and intend-ed to make preparations accordingly."

This ought not to be used (though it sometimes is, for shortness) to mean:

(2) "He replied ..., and he intended."

In (1), "intended," having no subject, must be supposed to be connected with the nearest preceding verb, in the same mood and tense, that has a subject, *i.e.* "wished." It follows that (1) is a condensation of:

(3) "He replied that he wished ..., and that he intended."

(2), though theoretically free from ambiguity, is practically ambiguous, owing to a loose habit of repeating the subject unnecessarily. It would be better to insert a conjunctional word or a full stop between the two statements. Thus:

(4) "He replied that he wished to help them, and *indeed* he intended," &c., or "He replied, &c. He intended, &c."

Where there is any danger of ambiguity, use (3) or (4) in preference to (1) or (2).

29. **When there are several infinitives, those that are dependent on the same word must be kept distinct from those that are not.**

"He said that he wished *to* take his friend with him *to* visit the capital and *to* study medicine." Here it is doubtful whether the meaning is—

"He said that he wished to take his friend with him,

(1)   *and also* to visit the capital and study medicine," or

(2)   "that his friend might visit the capital *and might also* study medicine," or

(3)   "on a visit to the capital, *and that he also* wished to study medicine."

From the three different versions it will be perceived that this ambiguity must be met (*a*) by using "that" for "to," which allows us to repeat an auxiliary verb [*e.g.* "might", and (*b*) by inserting conjunctions. As to insertions of conjunctions.

"In order to," and "for the purpose of," can be used to distinguish (wherever there is any ambiguity) between an infinitive that *expresses a purpose,* and an infinitive that does not, *e.g.* "He told his servant to call upon his friend, *to* (in order to) give him information about the trains, and not to leave him till he started."

30.   **The principle of suspense.** Write your sentence in such a way that, until he has come to the full stop, the reader may feel the sentence to be incomplete. In other words, keep your reader in *suspense.* Suspense is caused (1) by placing the "if-clause" first, and not last, in a conditional sentence; (2) by placing participles before the words they qualify; (3) by using suspensive conjunctions, *e.g. not only, either, part-ly, on the one hand, in the first place,* &c.

The following is an example of an *unsuspended* sentence. The sense *draggles*, and it is difficult to keep up one's attention.

"Mr. Pym was looked upon as the man of greatest experience in parliaments, | where he had served very long, | and was always a man of business, | being an officer in the Exchequer, | and of a good reputation generally, | though known to be inclined to the Puritan party; yet not of those furious resolutions (*Mod. Eng.* so furiously resolved) against the Church as the other leading men were, | and wholly devoted to the Earl of Bedford,—who had nothing of that spirit."

The foregoing sentence might have ended at any one of the eight points marked above. When suspended it becomes:—

"Mr. Pym, owing to his long service in Parliament in the Exchequer, was esteemed above all others for his Parliamentary experience and for his knowledge of business. He had also a good reputation generally; for, though openly favouring the Puritan party, he was closely devoted to the Earl of Bedford, and, like the Earl, had none of the fanatical spirit manifested against the Church by the other leading men."

30a. It is a violation of the principle of Suspense to introduce unexpectedly, at the end of a long sentence, some short and unemphatic clause beginning with (a) " ... not" or (b) " ... which."

   (a)   "This reform has already been highly beneficial to all classes of our countrymen, and will, I am persuaded, encourage among us industry, self-dependence, and frugality, *and not, as some say, wastefulness.*"

Write "not, as some say, wastefulness, but industry, self-dependence, and frugality."

(b) "After a long and tedious journey, the last part of which was a little dangerous owing to the state of the roads, we arrived safely at York, *which is a fine old town.*"

Exception

When the short final clause is intended to be unexpectedly unemphatic, it comes in appropriately, with something of the sting of an epigram. Thus:

"The old miser said that he should have been delighted to give the poor fellow a shilling, but most unfortunately he had left his purse at home—*a habit of his.*"

Suspense naturally throws increased emphasis on the words for which we are waiting, *i.e.* on the end of the sentence. It has been pointed out above that **a monotony of final emphasis is objectionable, especially in letter writing and conversation.**

31. **Suspense must not be excessive.** *Excess of suspense* is a common fault in boys translating from Latin. "Themistocles, having secured the safety of Greece, the Persian fleet being now destroyed, when he had unsuccessfully attempted to persuade the Greeks to break down the bridge across the Hellespont, hearing that Xerxes was in full flight, and thinking that it might be profitable to secure the friendship of the king, wrote as follows to him." The more English idiom is: "When Themistocles had secured the safety of Greece by the destruction of the Persian fleet, he made an unsuccessful attempt to persuade the Greeks to break down the bridge across the Hellespont. Soon afterwards, hearing &c."

A long suspense that would be intolerable in prose is tolerable in the introduction to a poem. See the long interval at the beginning of *Paradise Lost* between "Of man's first disobedience" and "Sing, heavenly Muse." Compare also the beginning of *Paradise Lost*, Book II.:

> *"High on a throne of royal state, which far*
> *Outshone the wealth of Ormuz and of Ind,*
> *Or where the gorgeous East with richest hand*
> *Showers on her kings barbaric pearl and gold—*
> *Satan exalted sat."*

with the opening of Keats' *Hyperion*:

> *"Deep in the shady sadness of a vale*
> *Far sunken from the healthy breath of morn,*
> *Far from the fiery noon and eve's one star—*
> *Sat grey-haired Saturn, quiet as a stone."*

32. In a long conditional sentence put the "if-clause," antecedent, or protasis, first.

Everyone will see the flatness of "Revenge thy father's most unnatural murder, if thou didst ever love him," as compared with the suspense that forces an expression of agony from Hamlet in—

> *"Ghost. If thou didst ever thy dear father love—Hamlet.*
> *O, God! Ghost. Revenge his foul and most unnatural murder."*

The effect is sometimes almost ludicrous when the consequent is long and complicated, and when it precedes the antecedent or "if-clause." "I should be delighted to introduce you to my friends, and to show you the objects of interest in our city, and the beautiful scenery in the neighbourhood, if you were here." Where the "if-clause" comes last, it ought to be very emphatic: "if you were *only* here."

The introduction of a clause with "if" or "though" in the middle of a sentence may often cause ambiguity, especially when a great part of the sentence depends on "that:" "His enemies answered that, for the sake of preserving the public peace, they would keep quiet for the present, though he declared that cowardice was the motive of the delay, and that for this reason they would put off the trial to a more convenient season."

33. Suspense[13] is gained by placing a Participle or Adjective that qualifies the Subject, before the Subject.

     "*Deserted* by his friends, he was forced to have recourse to those that had been his enemies." Here, if we write, "He, deserted by his friends, was forced &c.," *he* is unduly emphasized; and if we write, "He was forced to have recourse to his enemies, having been deserted by his friends," the effect is very flat.

     Of course we might sometimes write "He was deserted and forced &c." But this cannot be done where the "desertion" is to be not stated but implied.

Often, when a participle qualifying the subject is introduced late in the sentence, it causes positive ambiguity: "With this small force the general determined to attack the foe, *flushed* with recent victory and *rendered* negligent by success."

An excessive use of the *suspensive participle* is French and objectionable: *e.g.* "*Careless* by nature, and too much *engaged* with business to think of the morrow, *spoiled* by a long-established liberty and a fabulous prosperity, *having*for many generations forgotten

---

13. See (30).

the scourge of war, we allow ourselves to drift on without taking heed of the signs of the times." The remedy is to convert the participle into a verb depending on a conjunction: "Because we are by nature careless, &c.;" or to convert the participle into a verb co-ordinate with the principal verb, *e.g.* "*We are* by nature careless, &c., and therefore we *allow* ourselves, &c."

34. **Suspensive Conjunctions, e.g. "either," "not only," "on the one hand," add clearness.** Take the following sentence:—"You must take this extremely perilous course, in which success is uncertain, and failure disgraceful, as well as ruinous, or else the liberty of your country is endangered." Here, the meaning is liable to be misunderstood, till the reader has gone half through the sentence. Write *"Either* you must," &c., and the reader is, from the first, prepared for an alternative. Other suspensive conjunctions or phrases are *partly, for our part; in the first place; it is true; doubtless; of course; though; on the one hand.*

35. Repeat the Subject when the omission would cause ambiguity or obscurity. The omission is particularly likely to cause obscurity after a Relative standing as Subject:—

"He professes to be helping the nation, which in reality is suffering from his flattery, and (he? or it?) will not permit anyone else to give it advice."

The Relative should be repeated when it is the Subject of several Verbs. "All the pleasing illusions *which* made power gentle and obedience liberal, *which* harmonized the different shades of life, and *which*, by a bland assimilation, incorporated into politics the sentiments that beautify and soften private society, are to be dissolved by this new conquering empire of light and reason."

36.   **Repeat a Preposition after an intervening Conjunction, especially if a Verb and an Object also intervene.**

"He forgets the gratitude that he owes to those that helped all his companions when he was poor and uninfluential, and (*to*) John Smith in particular." Here, omit *to*, and the meaning may be "that helped all his companions, and John Smith in particular." The intervention of the verb and object, "helped" and "companions," causes this ambiguity.

37.   **When there are several Verbs at some distance from a Conjunction on which they depend, repeat the Conjunction.**[14]

"When we look back upon the havoc that two hundred years have made in the ranks of our national authors—and, above all, (*when*) we refer their rapid disappearance to the quick succession of new competitors—we cannot help being dismayed at the prospect that lies before the writers of the present day."

Here omit "when," and we at once substitute a parenthetical statement for what is really a subordinate clause.

In reporting a speech or opinion, "that" must be continually repeated, to avoid the danger of confusing what the writer says with what others say.

"We might say that the Cæsars did not persecute the Christians; (*that*) they only punished men who were charged, rightly or wrongly, with burning Rome, and committing the foulest abominations in secret assemblies; and (*that*) the refusal to throw frankincense on the altar of Jupiter was not the crime, but only evidence of the crime."

---

14.   The repetition of Auxiliary Verbs and Pronominal Adjectives is also conducive to clearness.

37a. Repeat Verbs after the conjunctions "than," "as," &c.

"I think he likes me better *than* you;" *i.e.* either "than you like me," or "he likes you."

"Cardinal Richelieu hated Buckingham as sincerely as *did* the Spaniard Olivares." Omit "did," and you cause ambiguity.

38. **If the sentence is so long that it is difficult to keep the thread of meaning unbroken, repeat the subject, or some other emphatic word, or a summary of what has been said.**

"Gold and cotton, banks and railways, crowded ports, and populous cities — *these* are not the elements that constitute a great nation."

This repetition (though useful and, when used in moderation, not unpleasant) is more common with speakers than with writers, and with slovenly speakers than with good speakers.

"The country is in such a condition, that if we delay longer some fair measure of reform, sufficient at least to satisfy the more moderate, and much more, if we refuse all reform whatsoever — I say, if *we adopt so unwise a policy, the country is in such a condition* that we may precipitate a revolution."

Where the relative is either implied (in a participle) or repeated, the antecedent must often be repeated also. In the following sentence we have the Subject repeated not only in the final summary, but also as the antecedent: —

"But if there were, in any part of the world, a national church regarded as heretical by four-fifths of the nation committed to its care; a *church* established and maintained by the sword; a *church* producing twice as many riots as conversions; a *church* which, though possessing great wealth and power, and though long backed by persecuting laws, had, in the course of many generations, been found unable to propagate its doctrines, and barely able to maintain its ground; a *church* so odious that fraud and violence, when used against its clear rights of property, were generally regarded as fair play; a *church* whose ministers were preaching to desolate walls, and with difficulty obtaining their lawful subsistence by the help of bayonets,— *such a church*, on our principles, could not, we must own, be defended."

39. **It is a help to clearness, when the first part of the sentence prepares the way for the middle and the middle for the end, in a kind of ascent. This ascent is called "climax."**

In the following there are two climaxes, each of which has three terms:—

"To gossip(a) is a fault(b); to *libel*(a'), a *crime*(b'); to slander(a"), a *sin*(b")."

In the following, there are several climaxes, and note how they contribute to the clearness of a long sentence:—

"Man, working, has *contrived*(a) the Atlantic Cable, but I declare that it *astonishes*(b) me far more to think *that for his mere amusement*(c), that to *entertain a mere idle hour*(c'), he has *created*(a') 'Othello' and 'Lear,' and I am more than astonished, I am *awe-struck*(b'), at that inexplicable elasticity of his nature which enables him, instead of *turning away*(d) from *calamity and grief*(e), or instead of merely *defying*(d') them, actually to *make them the material of his amusement*(d"), and to draw from the *wildest agonies of the human spirit*(e') a pleasure which is not only *not cruel*(f), but is in the highest degree *pure and ennobling*(f')."

The neglect of climax produces an abruptness that interferes with the even flow of thought. Thus, if Pope, in his ironical address to mankind, had written—

"Go, wondrous creature, mount where science guides;
Go, measure earth, weigh air, and state the tides;
Go, teach Eternal Wisdom how to rule"—

the ascent would have been too rapid. The transition from earth to heaven, and from investigating to governing, is prepared by the intervening climax—

"Instruct the planets in what orbs to run;
Correct old Time, and regulate the Sun;
Go, soar with Plato to th' empyreal sphere,
To the first good, first perfect, and first fair."

40. **When the thought is expected to ascend and yet descends, feebleness and sometimes confusion is the result. The descent is called "bathos."**

"What pen can describe the tears, the lamentations, the agonies, the *animated remonstrances* of the unfortunate prisoners?"

"She was a woman of many accomplishments and virtues, graceful in her movements, winning in her address, a kind friend, a faithful and loving wife, a most affectionate mother, and she *played beautifully on the pianoforte.*"

INTENTIONAL BATHOS has a humorous incongruity and abruptness that is sometimes forcible. For example, after the climax ending with the line—

"Go, teach Eternal Wisdom how to rule,"

Pope adds—

"Then drop into thyself, and be a *fool.*"

40a. **A new construction should not be introduced without cause.** A sudden and apparently unnecessary change of construction causes awkwardness and roughness at least, and sometimes breaks the flow of the sentence so seriously as to cause perplexity. Thus, write "virtuous and accomplished," or "of many virtues and accomplishments," not "of many virtues and accomplished;" "riding or walking" or "on foot or horseback," not "on foot or riding." In the same way, do not put adjectives and participles, active and passive forms of verbs, in too close juxtaposition. Avoid such sentences as the following:—

"He had good reason *to believe* that the delay was not *an accident* (accidental) but *premeditated*, and *for supposing* (to suppose, or else, for believing, above) that the fort, though strong both *by art* and *naturally* (nature), would be forced by the *treachery of the* governor and the *indolent* (indolence of the) general to capitulate within a week."

"They accused him of being *bribed* (receiving bribes from) by the king and *unwilling* (neglecting) to take the city."

41.   **Antithesis adds force, and often clearness.** The meaning of *liberal* in the following sentence is ascertained by the antithesis:—

"All the pleasing illusions which made *power*(a) *gentle*(b) and *obedience*(a') *liberal*(b') ... are now to be destroyed."

There is a kind of proportion. As *gentleness* is to *power*, so *liberality* (in the sense here used) is to *obedience*. Now *gentleness* is the check on the excess of power; therefore *liberal* here applies to that which checks the excess of obedience, *i.e.* checks servility. Hence *liberal* here means "free."

The contrast also adds force. "They aimed at the *rule*(a), not at the *destruction*(a'), of their country. They were men of great *civil*(b) and great *military*(b') talents, and, if the *terror*(c), the *ornament*(c') of their age."

Excessive antithesis is unnatural and wearisome:—

"Who can persuade where *treason*(a) is above *reason*(a'), and *might*(b) ruleth *right*(b'), and it is had for *lawful*(c) whatsoever is *lustful*(c'), and *commotioners*(d) are better than *commissioners*(d'), and *common woe*(e) is named common *wealth*(e')?"

42. **Epigram.** It has been seen that the neglect of climax results in lameness. Sometimes the suddenness of the descent produces amusement: and when the descent is intentional and very sudden, the effect is striking as well as amusing. Thus:—

(1) "You are not only not vicious, you are virtuous," is a *climax*.

(2) "You are not vicious, you are vice," is not *climax*, nor is it *bathos*: it is *epigram*.[15]

Epigram may be defined as a "short sentence expressing truth under an amusing appearance of incongruity." It is often antithetical.

"The Russian grandees came to { and diamonds," *climax*. court dropping pearls { and vermin," *epigram*.

"These two nations were divided { and the bitter remembrance by mutual fear { of recent losses," *climax*. { and mountains," *epigram*.

There is a sort of implied antithesis in:—

---

15. Professor Bain says: "In the epigram the mind is roused by a conflict or contradiction between the form of the language and the meaning really conveyed."

"He is full of information—(but flat also) like yesterday's *Times*."

"Verbosity is cured (not by a small, but) by a large vocabulary."

The name of epigram may sometimes be given to a mere antithesis; *e.g.* "An educated man should know something of everything, and everything of something."

43. **Let each sentence have one, and only one, principal subject of thought.**

"This great and good man died on the 17th of September, 1683, leaving behind him the memory of many noble actions, and a numerous family, of whom three were sons; one of them, George, the eldest, heir to his father's virtues, as well as to his principal estates in Cumberland, where most of his father's property was situate, and shortly afterwards elected member for the county, which had for several generations returned this family to serve in Parliament." Here we have (1) the "great and good man," (2) "George," (3) "the county," disputing which is to be considered the principal subject. Two, if not three sentences should have been made, instead of one. Carefully avoid a long sentence like this, treating of many different subjects on one level. It is called *heterogeneous*.

44. **The connection between different sentences must be kept up by Adverbs used as Conjunctions, or by means of some other connecting words at the beginning of each sentence.**—Leave out the conjunctions and other connecting words, and it will be seen that the following sentences lose much of their meaning:—

"Pitt was in the army for a few months in time of peace. His biographer (*accordingly*) insists on our confessing, that, if the young cornet had remained in the service, he would have been one of the ablest commanders that ever lived. (*But*) this is not all. Pitt (, *it seems,*) was not merely a great poet *in esse* and a great general *in posse*, but a finished example of moral excellence.... (*The truth is, that*) there scarcely ever lived a person who had so little claim to this sort of praise as Pitt. He was (*undoubtedly*) a great man. (*But*) his was not a complete and well-proportioned greatness. The public life of Hampden or of Somers resembles a regular drama which can be criticised as a whole, and every scene of which is to be viewed in connection with the main action. The public life of Pitt (, *on the other hand,*) is," &c.

The following are some of the most common connecting adverbs, or connecting phrases:

(1) expressing consequence, similarity, repetition, or resumption of a subject—*accordingly, therefore, then, naturally, so that, thus, in this way, again, once more, to resume, to continue, to sum up, in fact, upon this*;

(2) expressing opposition—*nevertheless, in spite of this, yet, still, however, but, on the contrary, on the other hand*;

(3) expressing suspension—*undoubtedly ... but; indeed ... yet; on the one hand ... on the other; partly ... partly; some ... others.*

Avoid a style like that of Bishop Burnet, which strings together a number of sentences with "and" or "so," or with no conjunction at all:

"Blake with the fleet happened to be at Malaga, before he made war upon Spain; *and* some of his seamen went ashore, *and* met the Host carried about; *and* not only paid no respect to it, but laughed at those who did." Write "*When* Blake &c."

45.   The connection between two long sentences sometimes requires a short intervening sentence, showing the transition of thought.

"Without force or opposition, it (chivalry) subdued the fierceness of pride and power; it obliged sovereigns to submit to the soft collar[16] of social esteem, compelled stern authority to submit to elegance, and gave a dominating vanquisher of laws to be subdued by manners. But now (*all is to be changed*:) all the pleasing illusions which made power gentle and obedience liberal, which harmonized the different shades of life, and which, by a bland assimilation, incorporated into politics the sentiments that beautify and soften private society, are to be dissolved by this new conquering empire of light and reason." If the words italicized were omitted, the transition would be too abrupt: the conjunction *but* alone would be insufficient.

* * * * *

BREVITY

46.   Metaphor is briefer than literal statement.

"The cares and responsibilities of a sovereign often disturb his sleep," is not so brief as "Uneasy lies the head that wears a crown," where the effect of care on the mind is assimilated to the effect of a heavy crown pressing on the head.

47.   General terms are briefer, though less forcible, than particular terms. Thus: "He devours *literature*, no matter of what kind," is shorter than, "Novels or sermons, poems or histories, no matter what, he devours them all."

---

16.   This metaphor is not recommended for imitation

47a. A phrase may be expressed by a word. "These impressions *can never be forgotten*, i.e. *are indelible*."

"The style of this book is *of such a nature that it cannot be understood*, i.e. *unintelligible*."

The words "of such a nature that" are often unnecessarily inserted.

48. Participles can often be used as brief (though sometimes ambiguous) equivalents of phrases containing Conjunctions and Verbs.

"*Hearing* (when he heard) this, he advanced." For more instances. So "phrases *containing* conjunctions" means "phrases *that contain* conjunctions." "*This done*, (for, *when this was done*) he retired."

Sometimes the participle "being" is omitted. "*France at our doors*, he sees no danger nigh," for "France being" or "though France is."

49. **Participles and participial adjectives may be used like Adjectives, as equivalents for phrases containing the Relative.**

"The never-*ceasing* wind," "the *clamouring* ocean," "the *drenching* rain," are instances. The licence of inventing participial adjectives by adding -*ing* to a noun, is almost restricted to poetry. You could not write "the *crannying* wind" in prose.

50. **A statement may sometimes be briefly implied instead of being expressed at length.** Thus, instead of "The spirit of Christianity was humanizing, and therefore &c.," or "Christianity, since it was (or being) of a humanizing spirit, discouraged &c.," we

can write more briefly and effectively, "Gladiatorial shows were first discouraged, and finally put down, by the *humanizing spirit of Christianity.*" So instead of "The nature of youth is thoughtless and sanguine, and therefore &c.," we can write, "The danger of the voyage was depreciated and the beauty of the island exaggerated by *the thoughtless nature of youth.*"

Sometimes a mere name or epithet implies a statement. "It was in vain that he offered the Swiss terms: war was deliberately preferred by the *hardy mountaineers,*" *i.e.* "by the Swiss, *because they were mountaineers and hardy.*" "The deed was applauded by all honest men, but the Government affected to treat it as murder, and set a price upon the head of (him whom they called) the *assassin.*" "*The conqueror of Austerlitz* might be expected to hold different language from *the prisoner of St. Helena,*" *i.e.* "Napoleon when elated by the victory of Austerlitz," and "Napoleon when depressed by his imprisonment at St. Helena."

CAUTION—Different names must not be used for the same person unless each of them derives an appropriateness from its context. Thus, if we are writing about Charles II., it would be in very bad taste to avoid repeating "he" by using such periphrases as the following: "The third of the Stewarts hated business," "the Merry Monarch died in the fifty-fourth year of his age," &c.

51.   **Conjunctions may be omitted.** The omission gives a certain forcible abruptness, *e.g.* "You say this: I (on the other hand) deny it."

When sentences are short, as in Macaulay's writings, conjunctions may be advantageously omitted.

Where a contrast is intended, the conjunction *but* usually prepares the way for the second of the two contrasted
terms: "He is good *but* dull." "Where *and* is used instead
of *but*, the incongruity savours of epigram: "He always talks
truthfully *and* prosily." "He is always amusing *and* false."

51a. **The Imperative Mood may be used for "if.**

"*Strip* (for, *if you strip*) Virtue of the awful authority
she derives from the general reverence of mankind, and
you rob her of half her majesty."

52. **Apposition may be used so as to convert two sentences into one.**

"We called at the house of a person to whom we had
letters of introduction, *a musician*, and, what is more,
a *good friend* to all young students of music." This is as
clear as, and briefer than, "He was a musician, &c."

53. **Condensation may be effected by not repeating (1)
the common subject of several verbs, (2) the common
object of several verbs or prepositions.**

(1) "He resided here for many years, and, after he had
won the esteem of all the citizens, (*he*) died," &c. So, (2) "He
came to, and was induced to reside in, this city," is shorter
than "He came to this city, and was induced to reside in it."

Such condensation often causes obscurity, and, even
where there is no obscurity, there is a certain harshness in
pausing on light, unemphatic words, such as *to, in*, &c., as
in the first example.

54. **Tautology**—The fault of repeating the same word
several times unnecessarily is called *tautology*, e.g.:

"This is a painful *circumstance*; it is a *circumstance* that I much *regret*, and he also will much *regret* the *circumstance*." But the fault is not to be avoided by

using different words to mean the same thing, as, "This is a painful *event*; it is a *circumstance* that I *much regret*, and he also will *greatly lament* the *occurrence*." The true remedy is to arrange the words in such a manner that there may be no unnecessary repetition, thus: "This is a painful circumstance, a circumstance that causes me, and will cause him, deep regret."

The repetition of the same meaning in slightly different words is a worse fault than the repetition of the same word. See, for examples, the extract from Sir Archibald Alison, at the end of the book. Thus *"A burning thirst* for conquests is a characteristic of this nation. It is an *ardent passion* that &c." Other instances are—"The *universal* opinion of *all* men;" "His judgment is so *infallible* that it is *never deceived*," &c.

55. **Parenthesis may be used with advantage to brevity.**

"We are all (and who would not be?) offended at the treatment we have received," is shorter and more forcible than the sentence would have been if the parenthesis had been appended in a separate sentence: "Who, indeed, would not be offended?"

Extreme care must, however, be taken that a parenthesis may not obscure the meaning of a long sentence.

56. **Caution: let clearness be the first consideration.** It is best, at all events for beginners, not to aim so much at being brief, or forcible, as at being perfectly clear. Horace says, "While I take pains to be brief, I fall into obscurity," and it may easily be seen that several of the rules for brevity interfere with the rules for clearness.

Forcible style springs from (1) vividness and (2) exactness of thought, and from a corresponding (1) vividness and (2) exactness in the use of words.

(1) When you are describing anything, endeavour to *see* it and describe it as you see it. If you are writing about a man who was killed, *see* the man before you, and ask, was he *executed, cut down, run through the body, butchered, shot,* or *hanged?* If you are writing about the capture of a city, was the city *stormed, surprised, surrendered, starved out,* or *demolished before surrender?* Was an army *repelled, defeated, routed, crushed,* or *annihilated?*

(2) Exactness in the use of words requires an exact knowledge of their meanings and differences. This is a study by itself, and cannot be discussed here.[17]

---

17. *See English Lessons for English People.*

3

EXERCISES

For an explanation of the manner in which these Exercises are intended to be used, see the Preface.

A number in brackets by itself, or followed by a letter, e.g. (43), (40 a), refers to the Rules.

Letters by themselves in brackets, e.g. (b), refer to the explanations or hints appended to each sentence.

N.B.—(10 a) refers to the first section of Rule (10); (10 a') to the Rule following Rule (10).

1.   "Pleasure and excitement had more attractions for him *than (a)* (36) (37 *a*) *his friend*, and the two companions became estranged (15 *a*) *gradually*."

(a) Write (1) "than for his friend," or (2) "than had his friend," "had more attractions than his friend."

2.   "(*a*) He soon grew tired of solitude even in that beautiful scenery, (36) the pleasures of the retirement (8) *which* he had once pined for, and (36) leisure which he could use to no good purpose, (*a*) (30) *being* (15) *restless by nature*."

(a) This sentence naturally stops at "purpose." Also "being restless" seems (wrongly) to give the reason why "leisure" could not be employed. Begin "Restless by nature...."

3. "The opponents of the Government are natural-
    ly, and not (*a*) (40 *a*) *without justification*, elated at
    the failure of the bold attempt to return two sup-
    porters of the Government at the recent election, (*b*)
    (10 *a'*) *which* is certainly to be regretted."

    (*a*) "unjustifiably." (*b*) Write, for "which," either (1) "an
attempt that &c.," or (2) "a failure that &c."

4. "Carelessness in the Admiralty departments has
    co-operated with Nature to weaken the moral power
    of a Government that particularly needs to be thought
    efficient in (*a*) (5) *this respect*, (*b*) (29) *to* counter-
    balance a general distrust of its excessive *desire* (*c*)
    (47 *a*) *to please everybody* in Foreign Affairs."

    (*a*) Write "the Navy." (*b*) Instead of "to" write "in order
to," so as to distinguish the different infinitives, (*c*) "obse-
quiousness."

5. "(*a*) He was sometimes supported by Austria, who,
    oddly enough, appears under Count Beust to have
    been more friendly to Italy *than* (37 *a*) *France*, (30) *in
    this line of action*."

    (*a*) Begin with "In this line of action." Why? (*b*) Write
"than was France" or "than France was."

6. "There was something so startling in (*a*) (5) *this* as-
    sertion, (*a*) (4) *that* the discoveries of previous inves-
    tigators were to be (*b*) (47 *a*) *treated as though they
    had never been made*, and (4) *that one who had not
    yet* (47 *a*) *attained the age of manhood* had super-
    seded the grey-headed philosophers (8) *who* had for
    centuries patiently sought after the truth, (4) *that* (*a*)
    (5) *it* naturally provoked derision."

(*a*) "This," "that," and "it," cause a little perplexity. Write "The startling assertion that the discoveries...." (*b*) "ignored." (*c*) "a mere youth," "a mere stripling."

7. "One of the recommendations (*on which very* (*a*) (26) (47, *a*) *much depended*) of the Commission was that a council in each province should establish smaller councils, each to have the oversight of a small district, and (*b*) (37) report to a central council on the state of Education in (*c*) (5) it."

(*a*) Write "cardinal recommendations." Derive "cardinal." (*b*) Write, either (1) "and should report," or (2) "and to report." (*c*) Write "in its province," or "district."

8. "At this (*a*) (1) *period* an (*b*) (11) *event* (*c*) (1) *transpired* that destroyed the last hopes of peace. The king fell from his horse and died two hours after the fall (*d*) (30), *which was occasioned by his horse's stumbling on a mole-hill, while he was on his return from reviewing his soldiers.*"

(*a*) What is a "period"? (*b*) Express the particular kind of event ("accident"). (*c*) What is the meaning of "transpired"? (*d*) Transpose thus: "While the king was on his return ... his horse ...; the king fell and &c." The cause should precede the effect.

9. "He determined (*c*) on selling all his estates, and, as soon as this was done (40 *a*), *to* (*c*) *quit* the country, (*a*) (33) believing that his honour demanded this sacrifice and (40) (40 *a*) *in* (*b*) *the* hope of satisfying his creditors."

(*a*) Begin with "Believing that &c." (*b*) "hoping thereby to satisfy &c." (*c*) "to sell" or "on quitting.".

10. "He read patiently on, Leading Articles, Foreign Correspondence, Money Article and all; (*a*) (43) during

which his father fell asleep, and he (*b*) went in search of his sister."

Point out the absurdity of "during which" applied to the last part of the sentence. (*a*) "Meanwhile." (*b*) Insert "then."

11. "The general was quite (*a*) (1) *conscious* (40 *a*) *how* treacherous were the intentions of *those who were* (*b*) (49) *entertaining* him, and (40 *a*) *of the* dangers from which he had *ecaped* (15) *lately*."

(*a*) Distinguish between "conscious" and "aware." (*b*) "entertainers."

12. "If *certain* (*a*) (11) *books* had been published a hundred years ago, there can be no doubt that *certain recent* (*b*) (11) *historians* would have made great use of them. But it *would* (*c*) (15 *b*) *not*, on that account, be judicious in a writer of our own times to publish an edition of the works of *one of these* (*b*) (11) *historians*, in which large extracts from these books should be incorporated with the original text."

(*a*) "Mrs. Hutchinson's Memoirs." (*b*) "Mr. Hume." (*c*) Add at the end of the sentence, "Surely not."

13. "He made no attempt to get up a petition, (32) though he did not like the new representative quite so well *as* (*a*) (37 *a*) *his colleagues*."

(*a*) "as did his colleagues" or "as he liked his colleagues."

14. "Though he was (*a*) (15) *obstinate* and (15) *unprincipled*, yet he could not face an angered father (15 *a*) *in spite of his effrontery*."

(*a*) Begin with "Obstinate."

15. "He was known to his country neighbours (*a*) (15) *during more than forty years* as a gentleman of cultivated mind, (40 *a*) *whose principles were high*, (40 *a*) *with polished address*, happy in his family, and (*b*) (40 *a*) *actively*discharging local duties; and (40 *a*) *among* political men, as an honest, industrious, and sensible member of Parliament, (40 *a*) *without* (*c*) *eagerness* to display his talents, (40 *a*) *who* (10 *g*) *was* stanch to his party, and attentive to the interests of *those whose* (*d*) (47 *a*) *representative he was.*"

(*a*) "During more &c.," is emphatic, and affects the latter as well as the former half of the sentence: hence it should stand first. (*b*) "in the discharge of." (*c*) "not eager." (*d*) Condense into one word.

16. "The poor think themselves no more disgraced by taking bribes at elections *than* (*a*) (37 *a*) *the rich* by offering them."

(*a*) Write (1) "Than the rich think themselves disgraced," or (2) "Than they think the rich disgraced."

17. "We are told that the Sultan Mahmoud, by his perpetual wars, (*a*) (41) and his tyranny, (*a*) (41) had filled his dominions with (*b*) (1) *misfortune and* (*c*) (11) *calamity*, and *greatly* (*d*) (11) *diminished* the population of the Persian Empire. *This great Sultan had* (*e*) (50) *a Vizier. We are not* (*f*) (55) (15) *informed* whether he was a humorist or an enthusiast, (*g*) *but he* pretended (*h*) that he had learned from (*i*) (11) *some one* how to understand the language of birds, so that *he* (*j*) (5) knew what was said by any bird that opened its mouth. (*k*) (44) One evening he was with the Sultan, returning from hunting. They saw a couple of owls *which* (10 *g*) *were* sitting

upon a tree (*l*) (8) *which* grew near an old wall out of a heap of rubbish. The Sultan said (6) he should like to know what the two owls were saying to one another, *and asked the* (*m*) *Vizier to* listen to their discourse and give him an account of it. The Vizier, (*n*) (31) pretending to be very attentive to the owls, approached the tree. He (*o*) returned to the Sultan and said that (6) he had heard part of their conversation, but did not wish to tell him what it was. (*p*) (5) *He*, not (*q*) (31) being satisfied with this answer, forced him to repeat everything the owls had said (20) *exactly*. (*r*) (44) (5) (6) *He* told (5) *him* that the owls were arranging a treaty of marriage between their children, and that one of them, after agreeing to settle five hundred villages upon the female owl, had prayed (6) that God would grant a long life to Sultan Mahmoud, because as long as he reigned over them they would never want ruined villages. The story says (*s*) *that* (*t*) (5) *he* was touched with the fable, (30) and (*s*) *that* he (*a*) (39) from that time forward *consulted* (15) *the good of his people*, and that he rebuilt the towns and villages (*v*) *which* had been destroyed."

(*a*) "abroad ... at home." (*b*) "ruin." (*c*) "desolation." (*d*) "half unpeopled." (*e*) "The Vizier of &c." (*f*) "We are not informed" is emphatic, and therefore should be inverted, "whether he was, &c., we are not informed." (*g*) "but he" will be omitted when "the Vizier" is made the subject of "pretended." (*h*) "Pretended" once meant "claimed," "professed." Write "professed." (*i*) "a certain dervish." (*j*) Introduce a new subject that you may substitute "Vizier" for "he," thus: "so that not a bird could open its mouth, but the Vizier knew &c." (*k*) "As he was, one evening, &c." (*l*) Note that the tree is represented as growing out of *ruins*. This is in accordance with the story of the mischief Mahmoud had done. (*m*) Omit this. (*n*) "Suspense" is out of place in a simple narrative like this; the sentence therefore ends with "owls." (*o*) "Upon his return." (*p*) "The Sultan" (*q*) "would not be satisfied." (*r*) "You must know then, &c." (*s*) Omit. (*t*) "so touched ... that." (*u*) end with "people." (*v*) Addison here uses "*which*" probably because of the preceding "that." We have to choose between sound and clearness. "Which" implies that *all* the villages in the country had been destroyed, whereas the country had been only (see above) "*half* unpeopled."

18. "Though this great king never permitted any pastime to interfere with the duties of state, which he considered to be *superior to* (54) *all other claims and of paramount importance*, and (*a*) (37) kept himself so far under control that he allowed no one pursuit or amusement to run to any excess, yet he *took* (54) *great pleasure in* the chase, *of which he was* (*b*) (2) *excessively* (54) *fond*, and for the purposes of which he created several *large* parks *of considerable* (54) *magnitude*."

(*a*) Either repeat "though," or else strikeout the first "though" and begin a new sentence after "excess." (*b*) Point out the contradiction between "excessively" and what precedes.

19. "To inundate (*a*) (11) their land, to man their ships, to leave their country, with all its miracles of art and industry, its cities, its villas, and its (*b*) (11) pastures buried under the waves (*c*) (11); to bear to a distant climate their (*d*) (11) faith and their old (*e*) (11) liberties; to establish, with auspices *that*(10 *a*) *might perhaps be happier*, the new (*f*) (11) *constitution of their commonwealth*, in a (*g*) (11) foreign and strange (*h*) (11) land, in the Spice Islands of the Eastern Seas, (38) were the plans which they had the spirit to form."

(*a*) Introduce "dykes." (*b*) Introduce something *peculiar* to the Dutch, *e.g.* "canals," "tulip gardens." (*c*) "of the German Ocean." (*d*) The Dutch were Calvinists. (*e*) The country was in old times "Batavia," so that "Batavian" would be a fit epithet to denote what the Dutch had inherited from their forefathers. (*f*) "Stadthaus," the German for "town-hall." (*g*) "other stars." (*h*) "strange vegetation."

20. "During twenty years of unexampled prosperity, *during* (*a*) *which* the wealth of the nation had shot (14 *a*) *up and extended its branches* on every side, and the funds *had* (14 *a*) *soared* to a higher point than had been ever attained before, (*b*) (15) speculation had become general."

(*a*) Omit. (*b*) Begin a new sentence: "This, *or* Prosperity, had increased the taste for speculation."

21. "At that time (*a*) (16) a mere narrow-minded pedant (for he deserves no better name) had been set up by the literary world as a great author, and as the supreme (*b*) critic, alone qualified to deliver decisions *which could never be* (*b*) *reversed* upon (15 *a*) *the literary productions of the day*."

(*a*) End with " ... one who was—for he deserves no better name—a mere narrow-minded pedant." (*b*) "Which could never be reversed" can be expressed in one word; or else "the supreme ... reversed" may be condensed into a personification: "a very Minos of contemporary criticism."

22. "With the intention of fulfilling his promise, and (40 *a*) *intending also* to clear himself from the suspicion that attached to him, he determined to ascertain *how* (40 *a*) *far this testimony* was corroborated, and (*a*) (40 *a*) the motives of the prosecutor, (*b*) (43) who had begun the suit last Christmas."

(*a*) "what were." (*b*) Begin a new sentence, "The latter &c.," or "The suit had been begun &c."

23. "The Jewish nation, relying on the teaching of their prophets, looked forward to a time when its descendants should be as numerous as *the heavenly* (11) *bodies*, and when the *products* (*a*) (11) *of the earth* should be *so increased as to create an abundant* (54) *plenty*, when each man should rest beneath the shade of his own (*a*) (11) *trees*, and when the *instruments* (11) *of war* should be *converted to the* (11) *uses of peace.*"

(*a*) Mention some "products," "trees" of Palestine.

24. "He replied (32), when he was asked the reason for his sudden unpopularity, that he owed it to his refusal to annul the commercial treaty, (*a*) (8) *which*(10 *a*) gave great displeasure to the poorer classes."

(*a*) Point out the ambiguity, and remove it by (8) or (10 *a*).

25. "I saw my old schoolfellow again by mere accident when I was in London at the time of the first Exhibition, (19) *walking* down Regent Street and looking in at the shops."

Point out and remove the ambiguity.

26. "He remained in the House while his speech was taken into consideration; *which* (52) *was* a common practice with him, because the debates amused his sated mind, and indeed *he used to say* (*a*) (6 *b*) *that they* were sometimes as good as a comedy. His Majesty had certainly never seen *a more* (17) *sudden turn* in any comedy of intrigue, either at his own

play-house or the Duke's, than that which this memorable debate produced."

(*a*) "and were sometimes, he used to say, as good &c."

27.   "The Commons would not approve the war (20) *expressly*, neither did they as yet condemn it (20) *expressly*, and (*a*) (18) the king might even have obtained a supply for continuing hostilities (19) from them, on condition *of* (*b*) *redressing* grievances *connected with the* (*c*) *administration of affairs at home*, among which the Declaration of Indulgence was a very *important* (*d*) (15_a_) one."

(*a*) Write "they were even ready to grant the king &c." (*b*) Use the verb with a subject, (*c*) Condense all this into one adjective, meaning "that which takes place at home." (*d*) End with a noun, "importance," or "foremost place."

28.   "Next to thinking clearly, (*a*) (5) *it is* useful to speak clearly, and whatever your position in life may hereafter be *it* cannot be such (54) as not to be improved by *this*, (*b*) so that *it* is worth while making almost any effort to acquire (*c*) *it*, if *it* is not a natural gift: (*d*) *it* being an undoubted (*d*) fact that the effort to acquire *it* must be successful, to some extent at least, if (*d*) *it* be moderately persevered in."

(*a*) "Next in utility ... comes speaking clearly—a power that must be of assistance to you &c." (*b*)" If, therefore, you cannot speak clearly by nature, you &c." (*c*) "this power." (*d*) Omit "fact;" "for undoubtedly, with moderate perseverance &c."

29.   "*It* (*a*) (38) *appears to me* (15) *a greater victory than Agincourt, a grander triumph of wisdom and faith and courage than even the English constitution or* (*b*) *liturgy*, to have beaten back, or even fought

against and stemmed in ever so small a degree, those *basenesses that* (*c*) (10_a_) *beset* human nature, which are now held so invincible that the influences of them are assumed as the fundamental axioms of economic science."

(*a*) Begin with "To have beaten &c.," and end with "liturgy." (*b*) Repeat for clearness and emphasis, "the English." (*c*) "The besetting basenesses of &c."

30. "The (*a*) (2) *unprecedented* impudence of our youthful representative reminds us forcibly of the *unblushing and* (54) (40) *remarkable* effrontery (*c*) (which (26) he almost succeeds in equalling) of the Member for St. Alban's, whom our (*b*) (1) *neophyte* (*b*) (1) *alluded to*, in the last speech with which he favoured *those whom* (47_a_) *he represents*, (19) as his pattern and example."

(*a*) Show that "unprecedented" is inconsistent with what follows. (*b*) What is the meaning of "neophyte," "alluded to"? (*c*) Begin a new sentence, "Our young adventurer &c.," and end with "and he almost succeeds in equalling his master."

31. "The (*a*) (1) *veracity* of this story is questionable, and there is the more reason for doubting the (*a*) (1) *truth* of the narrator, because in his remarks on the (1) *observation* of the Sabbath he distinctly (*a*) (1) *alludes to* a custom that can be shown never to have existed."

(*a*) Distinguish between "veracity" and "truth," "observation" and "observance." Show the inconsistency between "allude" and "distinctly."

32. "It (*a*) (5) is a most just distribution, (10 *a*) *which* the late Mr. Tucker has dwelt upon *so* (*b*) largely in his works, between pleasures in which we are passive,

and pleasures in which we are active. And I believe every attentive observer of human life will *assent to* (*c*) *this position*, that however (*d*) *grateful* the sensations may occasionally be in which we are passive, it is not these, but the latter class of our pleasures, (8) *which* constitutes satisfaction, (*e*) (38) *which* supply that regular stream of moderate and miscellaneous enjoyments in (10 *c*) *which* happiness, as distinguished from voluptuousness, consists."

(*a*) "There is great justice in &c." (b) Omit "so." (*c*) "admit." (*d*) Not often now used in this sense. (*e*) Repeat the antecedent, "I mean those (pleasures) &c."

33.   "The prince seemed to have before him a *limitless* (54) *prospect of unbounded* prosperity, carefully (33) *trained* for the (*a*) *tasks* of the throne, and stimulated by the (*a*) *pattern* of his father, (*b*) who (43) *breathed his* (3) *last*suddenly at the age of sixty-two, just after the conclusion of the war."

(*a*) Find more appropriate words. (*b*) Begin a new sentence.

34.   "On his way, he visited a son of an old friend (*a*) (25) *who* had asked *him* to call upon *him* on his journey northward. He (*b*) (5) was overjoyed to see *him*, and (*c*) *he* sent for one of *his* most intelligent workmen and told (*d*) *him*to consider *himself* at (*e*) *his* service, (30) as *he himself* could not take (*f*) *him* as *he* (*g*) wished about the city."

(*a*) If you mean that the "son" had "asked him," write "An old friend's son who;" if you mean that the "friend" had "asked him," write "He had been asked by an old friend to call, on his journey northward, upon his son. Accordingly he visited him on his way." (*b*) Use, instead of *he*, some name meaning "one who entertains others." (*c*) Use participle, (*d*) "The man." (*e*) "the stranger's." (*f*) "his guest." (*g*) Write "could have wished" to make it clear that "he" means "the host."

35. "Tillotson died in this year. He was exceedingly beloved both by King William and by Queen Mary (43), who nominated Dr. Tennison, Bishop of Lincoln, to succeed him."

36. "(*a*) The entertainment was arranged with a magnificence that was (*b*) perfectly *stupendous* and (*c*) *most unprecedented*, and which quite kept up his Lordship's *unrivalled* reputation for *unparalleled* hospitality, and, thanks to the *unequalled* energy of Mr. Smith, who is *rapidly becoming one of the most effective* toast-masters in the kingdom, the toasts were given with a spirit *quite unexampled* on occasions of this nature; and indeed we were forcibly reminded in this respect of the *inimitable* entertainment of three years ago (2)."

(*a*) Omit most of the epithets, or soften them down. Point out the contradictions in the sentence as it stands. (*b*) Write "a remarkable magnificence that quite &c.," thus dispensing with the following "and." (*c*) Show that "most" is superfluous.

37. "If we compare Shakespeare with the other dramatic authors of the Elizabethan era, *his wonderful superiority to them in the* (15) *knowledge of human nature* is *what* (15 *a*) *principally strikes us.*"

38. "The prince found himself at once in sore perplexity how to provide himself with the commonest comforts or even necessaries of life, when he landed on this desolate coast, being (33) accustomed to luxury."

39. "This make-shift policy recommended itself to the succeeding *ministers* (*a*) (50), *both because they were*

timid and because they were prejudiced, and they were delighted to *excuse* (*b*) (13) *themselves by quoting* the example of one who (*c*) (34) had controlled the Liberals and humoured the Conservatives, (37) commended himself to the country at large by his unfailing good-humour, and (*d*) (44) (37) done nothing worthy of the name of statesman."

(*a*) "to the timidity and prejudices of &c." (*b*) "shelter themselves behind." (*c*) "while he had at once." (*d*) "had yet done."

40. "William Shakespeare was the sun among the lesser lights of English poetry, and a native of Stratford-on-Avon (14 *a*)."

41. "(15 *b*) I think, gentlemen, you must confess that any one of you would have done the same (32), if you had been tempted as I was then, placed starving and ragged among wasteful luxury and comfort, deliberately instigated to acts of dishonesty by those whom I had been taught from infancy to love, (*a*) praised when I stole, mocked or punished when I failed to (15 *a*) *do* (*b*) *so*."

(*a*) Insert another infinitive beside "love." "Love" produces "obedience." (b) Repeat the verb instead of "do so."

42. "So far from being the first (54) *aggressor*, he *not* (22) *only* refused to prosecute his old friend when a favourable opportunity presented itself for revenging himself thus upon him, *but also* his friend's adviser, John Smith. Smith (*a*) *at all* (23) *events* suspected, if he did not know of the coming danger, and had given no information of it."

(*a*) If "at all events" qualifies "Smith," the sentence must be altered. "Yet, however innocent his friend may have been, at all events Smith suspected...." If the words qualify "suspected," place them after "suspected."

43. "It is quite true that he paid 5_s._ per day to English navvies, *and even 6s.*, (19) in preference to 2_s._ 6_d._ to French navvies."

44. "Having climbed to the *apex* of the Righi to enjoy the spectacle of the sun-rise, I found myself so *incommoded* by a number of *illiterate individuals* who had *emerged* from the hotel for a (*a*) (1) *similar* purpose, that I determined to quit them *at the earliest practicable period*; and therefore, without stopping to *partake of breakfast*, I *wended my way* back *with all possible celerity.*" (3)

    (*a*) "the same."

45. "You admit that miracles are *not natural*. Now whatever *is unnatural* is wrong, and since, by your own admission, miracles are *unnatural*, it follows that miracles are wrong." (1)

46. "Who is the man that has dared to call into *civilized* alliance the (*a*) (41) inhabitant of the woods, to delegate to the (*a*) Indian the defence of our disputed rights?

    (*a*) Insert some antithetical or other epithets.

47. "A (*a*) *very* (11) *small proportion* indeed of those who have attempted to solve this problem (*b*) (19) have succeeded in obtaining even a plausible solution."

    (*a*) State what proportion succeeded, or, if you like, what failed: "not one in a hundred." (*b*) Begin, "Of all those that &c."

48. "*To be suddenly* (*a*) (47 *a*) *brought into contact* with a system (8) *which* forces one to submit to wholesale

imposture, and *to being* (40 *a*) *barbarously ill-treat-ed*, naturally repels (*a*) (15 *a*) *one.*"

(*a*) Write, either (1) "Collision ... causes a natural re-pulsion," or (2) "When brought into contact ... one is natu-rally repelled," or (if "ill-treatment" is emphatic), (3) "One is naturally repelled by collision with &c."

49.   "We annex a letter recently addressed by Mr. — —'s direction to the Editor of the — —, in contradiction of statements, equally untrue, which appeared in that periodical, *and* (*a*) (9) *which* the editor has under-taken to insert in the next number.... I am sure that all must regret that statements *so* (*b*) (51) *utterly* er-roneous should have (*c*) (23) *first* appeared in a pub-lication of such high character."

(*a*) What the writer intended to express was that the editor had undertaken to insert, not the "statements," but the "contradiction." (*b*) Omit either "so" or "utterly." (*c*) "appeared first," or, "for the first time."

50.   "This is a book *which* (10 *a*) *is* short and amus-ing, *which* (10 *a*) *can be easily* (*a*) *understood*, *which* (10 *a*) is admirably adapted for *the pur-pose for which it* (*b*) *was* (54) *written*; and (10 *e*) *which* ought to be more popular than the last work *which* (10 *a*) *was* published by the same au-thor."

(*a*) Express "which can be understood" in one adjec-tive. (*b*) "Its purpose."

51.   "When thousands are *left* (19) without (40) *pity* and without (40) *attention* (19) on a field of battle, amid (40) the insults of an enraged foe and (40) the tram-pling of horses, while the blood from their wounds, freezing as it flows, binds them to the earth, and (40)

they are exposed to the piercing air, *it* (15 *a*) *must be indeed a painful scene."*

The whole sentence must be remedied by (40).

52.   "(*a*) The youth was naturally thoughtful, and disposed (19) besides by his early training—(31) which had been conducted with great care, the object of his parents being to *pave* (14) *his way* as far as possible over the *stormy* (14) *sea of temptation* and to *lead* him into the *harbour* of virtue—to a sincere (*b*) (1) *remorse* (19) for the (*b*) (1) *crimes* that he had committed in the sight of heaven, and also for his recent (*b*) (1) *sin* in breaking the laws of his country."

(*a*) First state the reasons for his being "disposed." "The youth was naturally thoughtful; moreover, his early training had been conducted with great care by his parents, whose &c. .... He was therefore disposed &c." (*b*) What is the difference between "remorse" and "repentance," between "sin" and "crime"?

53.   "(*a*) *One day* (54) *early in the morning,* the general was approached by a messenger, (30) in the midst of the *entanglements and perplexities* which had *unexpectedly surprised* him, when the *perilous hour of* (54) *danger* was at hand, and (37), in spite of their promises, even the tribes that were *well disposed* (54) *and friendly,* were threatening to *desert him, and* (54) *leave him to face the enemy* (*b*) (23) *alone."*

Condense the sentence by omitting some of the italicized words, *e.g.* (*a*) "Early one morning." (*b*) Though there is no real ambiguity (unless a wrong emphasis is placed on "enemy"), yet, in strictness, "alone" ought to qualify "enemy." Write therefore, "alone in the face of the enemy."

54. "*A man* (*a*) (10 *d*) *who* neglected the ordinary duties *of* life, and, immersed in study, devoted himself to grand plans for the benefit of mankind, (*b*) (44) *and* refused to provide for the wants of those dependent on him, and suffered his aged relatives to become paupers because he would not help them, (*c*) would, in my opinion, (34) be a bad man, and not altogether (*d*) (40 *a*) without hypocrisy."

(*a*) "If a man." (*b*) "if he refused," or "while he refused." (*c*) "such a man" or "he." (*d*) "to some extent a hypocrite."

55. "I cannot believe in the guilt of (*a*) *one* (*b*) (10 *e*) *who*, whatever may have been said to the contrary, can be shown, and has been shown by competent testimony proceeding from those who are said to have carefully examined the facts, *in spite* (23) *of many obstacles*, to have resisted all attempts to (29) induce him to leave his situation, (*c*) (29) to consult his own interests and to (29) establish a business of his own."

(*a*) "his guilt;" (*b*) (1) "for, whatever &c.... it can be shown by &c.... that, in spite of &c., he resisted." Or (2) insert "in spite ... obstacles" between "have" and "carefully." (*c*) (1) "for the purpose of consulting ... and establishing." Or (2) write "and to consult his own interests by establishing &c."

56. "We must seek for the origin of our freedom, (*a*) (37) prosperity, and (*a*) (37) glory, in *that and only* (*b*) *that*[18] portion of our annals, (30) though *it* (*c*) *is* sterile and obscure. The great English people was (*d*) *then* formed; the notional (*e*) *disposition* began (*d*) *then* to exhibit those peculiarities which it has ever since (*e*) *possessed*; and our fathers (*d*) *then* became emphatically islanders, (*f*) in their politics, (*a*)

---

18. That which treats of the thirteenth century.

feelings, and (*a*) manners, *and* (30 *a*) *not merely in their geographical position*."

(*a*) Repeat the Pronominal Adjective, (*b*) Express the emphatic "only that" by beginning the sentence thus: "It is in that portion of our annals &c." (*c*) Omit. (*d*) "It was then that &c." (*e*) Use words implying something more *marked* than "disposition," and more *forcible* than "possessed;" in the latter case, "retained." (*f*) Repeat "islanders."

57. "(*a*) He was *the universal* (54) *favourite of* (54) *all* (8) *who knew him*, and cemented many friendships at this period, (*a*) (33) (moving in the highest circle of society, and, *as he* (*b*) (50) *had a* (4 *a*) *certain property, being independent* of the profits of literature), and soon completely extinguished the breath of slander which at the outset of his career had threatened to sap the foundations of his reputation."

(*a*) Begin "Moving in &c." (*b*) "rendered independent of ... by &c." Show that Rule (14) is violated by the metaphors.

58. "The outward and material form of that city which, during the brief period *which* (10 *a*) *is* comprised in our present book, reached the highest pitch of military, artistic, and literary glory, *was of this* (*a*) (15) *nature*. The progress of *the* (*b*) (5) *first* has been already traced."

(*a*) Begin the sentence with "Such was." (*b*) By "the first" is meant "military glory."

59. "The detachment not only failed to take the fort, (30) spite of their numbers and the weakness of the garrison, but also to capture the small force that was encamped outside the town, and was, after some sharp fighting, driven back with inconsiderable loss."

Point out the ambiguity. Remedy it by inserting either "which," or "the assailants."

60.   "(*a*) (*b*) *Believing* that these reforms can *only* (*c*) (21) be effected as public opinion is prepared for them, and that (5) *this* will be more or less advanced in different localities, the Bill of the Association, (*a*) (31) which has been for *a* (3) *considerable period* in draft, and will be introduced in the next Session of Parliament, provides for *placing* (*d*) (3) *the control in regard to the points above-mentioned in the* (3) *hands* of the ratepayers of each locality; the power to be exercised through representative Licensing Boards to be periodically elected by them."

(*a*) Place the parenthesis first, as an independent sentence: "The Bill of the Association has been ... Parliament." (*b*) What noun is qualified by "believing?" Write "In the belief." (*c*) "effected only so far as they are in accordance with public opinion, which &c." (*d*) "it, or, the Bill provides that the ratepayers ... shall receive control ... and shall exercise this control."

61.   "I think they are very (1) *nice* persons, for they kept me amused for a *long* (*a*) (11) *time together* yesterday by their (1) *nice* stories all about *what they* (*b*) *have experienced* in Japan, where they had been for (*a*) *ever so long*, and (*c*) (43) where they said that the natives ripped up *their* (*d*) (5) *stomachs*."

(*a*) Mention some time. (*b*) "experiences" or "adventures." (*c*) "among other things, they told us &c." (*d*) "their own."

62.   "To contend for advantageous monopolies, which are regarded with a dislike and a suspicion (*a*) *which daily* (10 *a*) *increases*, (30) *however natural it may be*

to be annoyed at the loss of that which one has once possessed, (15 *a*) is *useless.*"

(*a*) A compound adjective can be used, including "daily."

63. "Upon entering the rustic place of entertainment to partake of some refreshment, my nerves were horrified by lighting on a number of boisterous individuals who were singing some species of harvest song, and simultaneously imbibing that cup which, if it cheers, also inebriates; and when, banished from their society by the fumes of the fragrant weed, I wended my way to the apartment which adjoined the one in which I had hoped to rest my weary limbs, I found an interesting assortment of the fairer sex, who were holding a separate confabulation apart from the revels of their rougher spouses."

Write "village inn," "next room," &c., for these absurd circumlocutions.

64. "When Burgoyne was born, in 1782, Napoleon and Wellington *were both boys* (11)."

Napoleon studied at Brienne, Wellington at Eton. Mention this, and, in order to imply the *boyhood*, call Wellington "Arthur Wellesley."

65. "An honourable friend of mine, who is now, I believe, near me—(38) to whom I never can on any occasion refer without feelings of respect, and, on this subject, (36) feelings of the most grateful homage; (38) whose abilities upon this occasion, as upon some former ones, are not entrusted merely to the perishable eloquence of the (*a*) day, but will live to be the admiration of that (*a*) hour when all of us are mute and most of us forgotten: (*b*) (38) has told you that pru-

dence *is* (52) the first of virtues, *and* (52) can never be used in the cause of vice."

(*a*) Though "of the day" is a recognized expression for "ephemeral" or "transitory," yet to use "day" for a short time, and "hour" for a longer, is objectionable. Write *moment* for *day.* Else write *future* for *hour.* (*b*) " —this gentleman has told &c."

66. "To see the British artisan and his wife on the Sabbath, neat and clean and cheerful, with their children by their sides, (*a*) (19) *disporting* themselves under the open canopy of heaven, *is* (15) *pleasant.*"

(*a*) There is no reasonable ground for mistaking the sense here, as the context makes it clear; but since Lord Shaftesbury was questioned whether he meant *disporting* to qualify "artisan and his wife" or "children," write "and, by their sides, their children disporting &c."

67. "Even if (*a*) *it were* attended with extenuating circumstances, such conduct would deserve severe reprobation, (*b*) *and it* is the more called for because *it* would seem that (*c*) *it* was the intention of *the author of the crime,* in perpetrating (*e*) *it,* to inflict all the misery that was possible, upon his victim."

(*a*) Omit "it were." (*b*) "which." (*c*) "to have been." (*d*) Express "author of the crime" in one word. (*e*) Use the noun.

68. "The (*a*) (1) *observance* of the heavenly bodies must have been attended with great difficulties, (*b*) (30) before the telescope was (*a*) (1) *discovered,* and it is not to be wondered at if the investigations of astronomers were often unsatisfactory, and failed to produce complete (*a*) (1) *persuasion,* (30) (15, *a*) under these disadvantages."

(*a*) What is the difference between "observance" and "observation," "discover" and "invent," "persuasion" and "conviction"? (*b*) Begin "Before &c."

69. "He plunged into the sea once more, (30) not content with his previous exertions. After a long and dangerous struggle, he succeeded in reaching a poor woman that was crying piteously for help, and (*a*) (35) was at last hauled safely to shore."

(*a*) Point put and remedy the ambiguity by inserting "he" or by writing "who," according to the meaning.

70. "Sir John Burgoyne himself, face to face with Todleben, became (*a*) (1) *conscious* of the difference between the fortifications of San Sebastian and of Sebastopol, (*b*) *which* (10 *e*) was (*c*) (12) *very weak* compared with Metz or Paris."

(*a*) What is the exact meaning of *conscious*? (*b*) Avoid the relative, by repeating the name, with a conjunction, (*c*) "weakness itself."

71. "Upon Richard's leaving the (*c*) stage, the Commonwealth was again set up; and the Parliament which Cromwell had (*a*) *broken* was brought together; but the army and they fell into new disputes: so they were again (*a*) *broken* by the army: and upon that the nation was like to fall into (*b*) (11) *great* convulsions."

(*a*) Modern Eng., "broken up." (*b*) "violently convulsed." (*c*) It is a question whether this metaphor is in good taste. The meaning is that Richard "retired from public life." It might be asserted that Richard, the Commonwealth, the Parliament are regarded as so many puppets on a "stage." But this is extremely doubtful. Make *Parliament* the principal subject: "When Richard retired ... and when the Commonwealth &c.... the Parliament was ... but, falling into a dispute with &c., it was...."

72. "What a revolution in the military profession! He began with (*a*) (11) *unnecessary formality*, and (*b*) (11) *inefficient weapons*, and ended with (*c*) (*b*) (11) *greatly improved fire-arms.*"

(*a*) "pig-tail and pipe-clay." (*b*) "Six-pounders and flint-locks" are now inefficient compared with "twenty-four-pounders and breech-loaders." (*c*) Something is wanted antithetical to (*a*), perhaps "loose drill" or "open order."

73. "Children fear to go in the dark. Men fear death in the same way. The fear of children is increased by tales. So is the fear of death. The contemplation of death, as the 'wages of sin,' and passage to another world, is holy and religious. The fear of it, as a tribute due unto nature, is weak. In religious meditations on death there is sometimes mixture of vanity and of superstition."

Insert connecting adverbs or conjunctions.

74. "I have often heard him *reiterate* (54) *repeatedly* that he would never again, if a *safe* (54) *and secure path* was open to him, prefer the *perilous* (54) *road of danger*, however *alluring* (54) *and attractive* the latter might be."

75. "I thought in my dream that when my friend asked me whether I did not observe anything curious in the conduct of the pigeons, I (*a*) (4 *a*) *remarked* that if any one of the birds was so bold as to take an atom from a heap of grain in the midst of them, (31) (which (*b*) a detachment guarded, and which, being continually increased and never eaten, seemed useless), all

the rest turned against him and pecked him to death for the (c) (50) *action.*"

(a) Point out the ambiguity. (b) This should come earlier in the sentence, and not as a parenthesis. "I noticed a heap of grain in the midst of them, guarded by ... Being continually ..., to all appearance, useless: yet." (c) "theft."

76. "If this low view of the royal office becomes generally adopted, then sovereigns *who* (8) have always hitherto commanded the respect of Englishmen will by degrees fall into disrespect."

Point out the ambiguity. Show how it might be removed (a) by punctuation, (b) by altering "who."

77. "I struck the man in self-defence. I explained this to the magistrate. He would not believe me. Witnesses were called to support my statements. He committed me to prison. He had the right to do this. It is a right that is rarely exercised in such circumstances. I remonstrated."

Insert conjunctions or connecting adverbs.

78. "He attained a very distinguished position by mere (15) perseverance and common sense, which (52) (10 a) qualities are perhaps mostly underrated, (30) though he was deficient in tact and not remarkable for general ability."

79. "*Vindictiveness, which* (a) (50) *is a fault,* (b) *and* which may be defined as *anger* (10 a) *which is caused* not by sin nor by crime but by personal injury, ought to be carefully distinguished from *resentment, which* (a) (50) *is a virtue,* (b) *and* which is *anger* (49) *which is natural and* (c) *right* caused by an act (d) which is unjust, because it is unjust, (30 a) not because it is inconvenient."

(a) "The fault of vindictiveness;" "the virtue of resentment." (b) Omit (c) "Right" cannot be used as an adjective, but "righteous" can. (d) "an act of injustice."

80. "(a) He told his friend that (a) *his* brother was surprised that (a) *he* had given so small a contribution, for (a) *he* was (b) (12) *a very rich man*, in spite of (a) *his* recent losses and the bad state of trade, (19) (30) compared with himself."

(a) Use (6). (b) What Asian king was proverbial for wealth?

81. "(a) (15 b) It must be indeed wrong to (a) *crucify* a Roman citizen if to (b) (32) *slay* one is almost parricide, to (b) *scourge* him is a monstrous crime, and to (b) *bind* him is an outrage."

(a) "What must it be...?" (b) See (40).

82. "The *universal* (54) *opinion of all the* citizens was that the citadel *had been* (15) *betrayed*, (30) having been captured in broad daylight by a very small number of the enemy, and those unprovided with scaling ladders, and admitted by a postern gate, (15 a) and much wearied by a long march."

In any case "betrayed" must come at the end of a sentence. The sentence may be converted into two sentences: "The citadel had been captured.... Naturally therefore ...;" or, "The opinion ... for it had been captured...." Else, if one sentence be used, write "As the citadel had been captured &c."

83. "This author surpassed all *those who were living* (a) *at the same time with him* in the *forcible* (b) *manner in* which he could *address* (c) *an* appeal to the popular sympathy, and in the ease with

which he could *draw towards* (*a*) *himself* the hearts of his readers."

(*a*) Express in one word. (*b*) "force with." (*c*) Omit.

84. "This great statesman was indeed a pillar of commerce, and a star in the financial world. He guided or impelled the people from the quicksands of Protection and false political economy to the safe harbour of Free Trade; and (*a*) (14 *a*) saved the country several millions."

(*a*) It would be well to literalize the preceding metaphors. Else the literal statement must be changed into a metaphor.

85. "The ministers were most unwilling to meet the Houses, (*a*) (43) (51) *because* even the boldest of them (though their counsels were *lawless* (15) *and desperate*) had too much value for his (*b*) (11) *personal safety* to think of resorting to the (*c*) (12) unlawful modes of extortion that had been familiar to the preceding age."

(*a*) Begin a new sentence with "Lawless and desperate though their counsels had been &c." (*b*) "neck." (*c*) Insert some of these unlawful modes, "benevolences, ship-money, and the other &c."

86. "*We will not* (*a*) (15) *pretend to guess what* our grandchildren may think of the character of Lord Byron, as exhibited *in* (15 *a*) *his poetry.*" No writer ever had the whole eloquence of scorn, misanthropy, *and* (*a*) (15) *despair* (15 *a*) *so completely at his command.* That *fountain* (*b*) (12) *of bitterness* was never dry."

(*a*) "We will not pretend to guess" and "despair" are intended by the author to be emphatic. (*b*) "Marah."

87.   "The captain asked to be allowed fifty men, a supply of food, and one hundred and fifty breech-loaders. (44) The general replied coldly that he could not let his subordinate have (*a*) (4) *anything* that he wanted. (44) The captain was forced to set out (34) with an insufficient force, spite of the superabundance of soldiers doing nothing in the camp (34), and with every obstacle put in his way by a general who from the first had resolved not even to give him ordinary assistance, (*b*) (10 *a'*) *which* the captain had for some time anticipated."

(*a*) Point out and remove the ambiguity. (*b*) Write, according to the meaning, " ... assistance that" or " ... a resolution that."

88.   "I am a practical man, and disbelieve in everything (8) *which* is not practical; theories (*a*) *which* amuse philosophers and pedants have no attractions for me, (30) *for this reason*."

(*a*) What difference in the meaning would be caused by the use of "that" for the second "which"?

89.   "Yet, when that discovery drew no other severity but the (11 *a*) *turning* (*a*) *him out of office,* and *the* (11 *a*) *passing a sentence* (*b*) *condemning him to die for it* (31) (which was presently pardoned, and he was after a short confinement restored to his liberty), all men *believed* that the king knew of the letter, (*c*) (43) and that (6 *b*) the pretended confession of the secretary was only collusion to lay the jealousies of the king's (*d*) (11 *a*) *favouring* popery, (*e*) (43) which still hung upon him, (30) notwithstanding his (*e*) *writing* on the Revelation, and his (*e*) *affecting* to enter on all occasions into controversy, (*e*) *asserting* in particular that the Pope was Antichrist."

(*a*) "expulsion from." (*b*) "a pretended sentence to death — a pretence that was soon manifested by his pardon and liberation." (*c*) Begin a new sentence: "'The secretary's pretended confession,' it was said, 'was &c.'" (*d*) "the suspicion that the king favoured Popery." (*e*) The juxtaposition of the two verbal nouns, "writing" and "affecting," with the participle "asserting," is harsh. Write, "For, notwithstanding that he affected controversy, and attacked the Pope as Antichrist in his treatise on the Book of Revelation, the king was still suspected."

90. "The opinion that the sun is fixed was once too (*a*) (1) *universal* to be easily shaken, and a similar prejudice has often (*b*) *rendered* the progress of new inventions (15 *a*) *very slow*, (19) arising from the numbers of the believers, and not (36) the reasonableness of the belief."

(*a*) Write "general." Show the absurdity of appending "too" to "universal." (*b*) What single word can be substituted for "rendered slow"?

91. "The rest of the generals were willing to surrender unconditionally, (30) *depressed by this unforeseen calamity*; (4) *only* the young colonel, who retained his presence of mind, represented to them that they were increasing the difficulties of a position in itself very difficult (19) (15, *a*) *by their conduct*."

92. "To (*a*) (31) *an author who* is, in his expression of any sentiment, wavering between *the* (*b*) *demands of* perspicuity and energy (of which *the* (*c*) (40 *a*) *former of course* requires the first care, lest (40 *a*) he should fail of both), and (37) doubting whether the (*d*) phrase *which* (8) *has* (*e*) *the* most force and brevity will be (*f*) readily *taken* (*g*) *in, it may* (*h*) (3) *be recommended to use* both (*d*) expressions; first, (*h*) *to*

expound the sense sufficiently to be clearly understood, and then (*i*) *to* contract it into the most compendious and striking form."

(*a*) Write "When an author &c." (*b*) Can be omitted. (*c*) Assimilate the constructions: "Of which the former must, of course, be aimed at first, lest both be missed." (*d*) Use "expression" or else "phrase" in *both* places. (*e*) Assimilate the construction to what follows; write "that is most forcible and brief." (*f*) Insert "also." (*g*) "understood." (*h*) "let him use ...; first let him expound." (*i*) Omit.

93.   "When I say 'a great man,' I *not* (22) *only* mean a man intellectually great but also morally, (38) *who* (8) has no preference for diplomacy (*a*) (23) *at all events which* (10 *a*) *is* mean, petty, and underhanded to secure ends *which* (8) can be secured by an honest policy *equally* (20) *well*, (38) *who* (8) does not resemble Polonius, (*b*) who prefers to get at truth by untruthful tricks, and (*b*) who considers truth a carp *which* (10 *g*) *is* to be caught by the bait falsehood. We cannot call a petty intriguer great (*c*), (30) though we may be forced to call an unscrupulous *man by that* (15 *a*) *name*."

(*a*) "at all events no preference." (*b*) Why is *who* right here? If you like, you can write, "does not, like Polonius, prefer ... and consider." (*c*) End with "we cannot give the name to a petty intriguer."

94.   "I regret that I have some (*a*) (3) *intelligence which* (10 *a*) *is of a most* (3) *painful nature*, and which I must tell you at once, though (*b*) *I should like to defer it* on (*c*) (40 *a*) account of your ill-health, and *because* (*c*) (40 *a*) *you have already had* many troubles, and (40 *a*) *owing to* the natural dislike *which* (8) a friend must always feel to

say *that* (10 *f*) *which* is unpleasant. Many old friends in this district have turned against you: I scarcely like to write the words: *only* (21) I remain faithful to you, and I am sure you will believe that I am doing *that* (10 *f*) *which* is best for your interests."

(*a*) "news." (*b*) In a letter these words should remain is they are; but if a *period* is desired, they must (30) come last, after "unpleasant." (*c*) Write "because of your ill-health ... and the troubles ... and because of...."

95. "The general at once sent back word that the enemy had suddenly appeared on the other side of the river, and [(35) or (37)] then (*a*) retreated. (*b*) *It* was thought that (*b*) *it* would have shown more (*c*) (1) *fortitude* on his (3) *part* if he had attacked the fortifications, (*d*) *which* were not tenable for more than a week at all events. Such was the (54) *universal* opinion, *at* (23) *least, of* (54) *all* the soldiers."

(*a*) Point out the ambiguity. (*b*) "It was thought he would have shown &c." (*c*) Distinguish between "fortitude" and "bravery." (*d*) What would be the meaning if "that" were substituted for "which"? It will be perhaps better to substitute for "which," "since they."

96. "A notion has sprung up that the Premier, though he can legislate, cannot govern, and has attained an influence which renders it imperative, if this Ministry is to go on, that (*a*) *it* should be dispersed."

(*a*) Who or what "has attained"? Write "and this notion has become so powerful that, unless it is dispersed...."

97. "Those who are *habitually silent* (*a*) (3) *by disposition* and morose are less liable to the fault of exaggerating than those who are *habitually* (*a*) (3) *fond of talking*, and (40 *a*) *of* (*a*) (3) *a pleasant disposition*."

(a) Each of these periphrases must be condensed into a single adjective.

98. "This author, (a) (31) though he is not (b) *altogether* (c) *guiltless of* (b) *occasional* (c) *faults* of exaggeration, which are to be found as plentifully in his latest works as in *those which he* (d) *published when he was beginning his career as an author*, yet, *notwithstanding these* (e) *defects*, surpassed all *those who were living at the* (f) *same time with him* in the *clear* (g) *manner in* which he could, as it were, see into the feelings of the people at large, and in the power—*a power that indeed could not be* (f) *resisted*—with which he *drew* (f) *toward himself* the sympathy of *those who* (f) *perused his works.*"

(a) Convert the parenthesis into a separate sentence. (b) One of these words is unnecessary. (c) One of these is unnecessary. (d) Condense: "his earliest." (e) Omit these words as unnecessary. (f) Express all this in one word. (g) "clearness with."

99. "*Among the North* (a) (23) *American Indians* I had indeed heard of the perpetration of similar atrocities; but it seemed intolerable that such things should occur in a civilized land: and I rushed from the room at once, leaving the wretch where he stood, with his tale half told, (30) *horror-stricken at his crime.*"

(a) Make it evident whether the speaker once *lived* among the North American Indians, or not, and show who is "horror-stricken."

100. "His (1) *bravery* under this painful operation and the (1) *fortitude* he had shown in heading the last charge in the recent action, (30) *though he was* wounded at the time and had been unable to use his right arm, and was the only officer left in his regiment, out of

twenty who were alive the day before, (19) inspired every one with admiration."

Begin, "Out of twenty officers &c.... Though wounded &c.... he had headed." "The bravery he had then shown and...."

101. "*Moral* as well as (41) *other* considerations must have weight when we are selecting an officer (*a*) *that* (10 *b*) *will be placed in* a position that will task his intelligence (*b*) (18) *and his fidelity.*"

(*a*) The repetition of "that" is objectionable. Use "to fill." (*b*) "and" can be replaced by some other conjunction to suit what precedes.

102. "It happened that at this time there were a few Radicals in the House *who* (8) could not forgive the Prime Minister for being a Christian."

Point out the difference of meaning, according as we read "who" or "that."

103. "*It cannot be doubted* (15 *b*) *that* the minds of a vast number of men would be left poor shrunken things, full of melancholy and indisposition, and unpleasing to themselves, if (32) there were taken out of men's minds vain opinions, false valuations, imaginations as one (*a*) would, and *the* (15 *a*) *like.*"

(*a*) The meaning (which cannot easily be more tersely expressed than in the original) is "castles in the air," "pleasant fancies."

104. "God never wrought a miracle to refute atheism, because His ordinary works refute it. (*a*) A little philosophy inclines man's mind to atheism: depth in philosophy brings men's minds back to religion. (44) While the mind of man looks upon second causes

scattered, it may sometimes rest in them; (44) when it beholds the chain of them confederate and linked together, it must needs acknowledge a Providence. (44) That school which is most accused of atheism most clearly demonstrates the truth of religion."

(*a*) Insert a suspensive conjunction.

105. "The spirit of Liberty and the spirit of Nationality were once for all dead; (*a*) (5) *it* might be for a time a pious duty, but it could not continue always *expedient or* (*c*) (15) (18) *profitable to* (*b*) (13) *mourn* (*c*) (15 *a*) *for their loss.* Yet this is the (*b*) (13) *feeling* of the age of Trajan."

(*a*) Omit. (*b*) "To sit weeping by their grave;" "attitude." (*c*) Notice that "expedient or profitable" are emphatic, as is shown by "yet" in the next sentence. Make it evident therefore, by their position, that these words are more emphatic than "to mourn &c."

106. "(*a*) *If we ask* (15 *b*) what was the nature of the force by which this change was effected, (*a*) *we find it to have been* (*b*) the force that had seemed almost dead for many generations—(38) of theology."

(a) Omit these words. (b) Begin a new sentence: "It was a force &c."

107. "I remember Longinus highly recommends a description of a storm by Homer, because (*a*) (5) (*c*) *he* has not amused himself with little fancies upon the occasion, as authors of an inferior genius, whom he mentions, (*b*) (15 *a*) have done, (30) *but* (*c*) *because* he has gathered together those (*d*) (1) *events* which are the most apt to terrify the imagination, and (35) really happen in the raging of a tempest."

(*a*) "The poet." (*b*) Omit "have done" and write "like some authors." (*c*) Suspend the sentence by writing "the poet ... instead of ... has." (*d*) What is the word for "that which happens *around* one, or in connection with some central object?"

108. "To have passed (*a*) (3) *in a self-satisfied manner* through twenty years of office, letting things take their own course; to have (*b*) *sailed* with consummate sagacity, never against the tide of popular (*c*) *judgement*; to have left on record as the sole title to distinction among English ministers a peculiar art of (*d*) *sporting with* the heavy, the awful responsibility of a nation's destiny with the jaunty grace of a juggler (11) (*e*) *playing with* his golden ball; to have joked and intrigued, and bribed and (*f*) *deceived*, with the result of having done nothing (*g*), (*h*) *either* for the poor, (*h*) *or* for religion (for (*i*) which indeed he did worse than nothing), (*h*) *or* for art and science, (*h*) *or* for the honour or concord or even the financial prosperity of the nation, (38) is surely a miserable basis on which the reputation of a great (15) statesman *can be* (*k*) (15 *a*) *founded*."

(*a*) "complacently." (*b*) "Sail" implies will and effort: use a word peculiar to a helpless ship, so as to contrast paradoxically with "sagacity." (*c*) Use a word implying less thought and deliberation. (*d*) *With* is too often repeated; write "bearing" so as to introduce the illustration abruptly. (*e*) "tossing." (*f*) Use a word implying a particular kind of "deceit," not "lying," but the next thing to "lying." (*g*) Insert the word with a preceding and intensifying adverb, "absolutely nothing." (*h*) Instead of "either," "or," repeat "nothing." (*i*) The parenthesis breaks the rhythm. Write "nothing, or worse than nothing." (*k*) "to found."

109.   "A glance at the clock will make you (1) *conscious* that
it is nearly three in the morning, and I therefore ask
you, gentlemen, instead of wasting more time, to put
this question to yourselves, 'Are we, or are we not,
here, for the purpose of (1) *eliminating* the truth?'"

110.   "The speech of the Right Honourable member, so far
from *unravelling* (14) *the obscurities of this knotty
question,* is eminently calculated to mislead his supporters (*a*) (8 *a*) *who* have not made a special study
of it. It may be (*b*) (23) *almost* asserted of every statement (8) *which* he has made that the very (1) *converse* is the fact."

(*a*) The meaning appears to be, not "*all* his supporters," but "*those of* his supporters who:" the convenience of
writing "his supporters *that*" is so great that I should be
disposed to use "that." (*b*) "Every," not "asserted," requires
the juxtaposition of "almost."

111.   "The provisions of the treaty *which* (8) require the
consent of the Parliament of Canada await its as-
sembling."

Point out the meaning conveyed by *which,* and by *that.*

112.   "Mrs. Smith demonstrated (26), in opposition to the
general dictum of the press, that (*a*) *there had been* a
reaction against woman's suffrage, that there had
really been a gain of one vote in the House of Commons."

(*a*) Substitute "instead of," and erase the second "that."

113.   "The practice of smoking hangs like a gigantic (14 *a*)
cloud of evil over the country."

4

CONTINUOUS EXERCISES

CLEARNESS

The following exercises consist of extracts from Burnet, Butler, and Clarendon, modernized and altered with a view to remove obscurity and ambiguity. The modernized version will necessarily be inferior to the original in unity of style, and in some other respects. The charm of the author's individuality, and the pleasant ring of the old-fashioned English, are lost. It is highly necessary that the student should recognize this, and should bear in mind that the sole object is to show how the meaning in each case might have been more *clearly* expressed.

Occasionally expressions have been altered, not as being in themselves obscure or objectionable, but as indicating a habit of which beginners should beware. For example, in the extract from Burnet, *he* is often altered, not because, in the particular context, the pronoun presents any obscurity, but because Burnet's habit of repeating *he* is faulty.

These exercises can be used in two ways. The pupil may either have his book open and be questioned on the reasons for each alteration, or, after studying the two versions, he may have the original version dictated to him, and then he may reproduce the parallel version, or something like it, on paper.

LORD CLARENDON

The principal faults in this style are, long heterogeneous sentences (43), use of phrases for words (47, a), ambiguous use of pronouns (5), excessive separation of words grammatically connected together (19).

ORIGINAL VERSION. PARALLEL VERSION

(44) It will not be impertinent And now, in order to explain, as nor *unnatural to this* (50) far as possible, how so prodigious *present discourse*, to set down an alteration could take place in in this place the present temper so short a time, and how the[19] and constitution of both Houses royal power could fall so low as of Parliament, and (34) of the to be unable to support itself, court itself, (30) that (5) *it* its dignity, or its faithful may be the less wondered at, that servants, it will be of use to set so prodigious an alteration should down here, where it comes most be made in so short a time, and naturally, some account of the[20] (37) the crown fallen so low, that present temper and composition, it could neither support itself not only of both Houses of nor its own majesty, nor *those Parliament, but also of the court who would* (47 a) *appear itself. faithful to it.*

* * * * * * * * * *

(Here follows a description of the House of Lords.)

In the House of Commons were many In the House of Commons persons of wisdom and gravity, who there were many men of wisdom (7) *being possessed* of great and and

---

19. The original metaphor uses the crown as a prop, which seems a confusion. Though the metaphor is so common as scarcely to be regarded as a metaphor, it is better to avoid the appearance of confusion.
20. We sometimes say, briefly but not perhaps idiomatically, "the *then* sovereign," "the *then* temper," &c.

judgment whose high plentiful fortunes, though they position and great wealth disposed were undevoted enough
to the them, in spite of their indifference court, (19) had
all imaginable to the court, to feel duty for the king, and
affection a most loyal respect for the to the government *established*(47 king, and a great affection for *a*) *by law* or
ancient custom; the ancient constitutional (43) and without doubt, the *major government of the country.* Indeed,
part of that (54) *body* it cannot be doubted that consisted
of men who had no mind the majority had no intention
to to break the peace of the kingdom, break the peace of
the kingdom or to make any considerable or to make any
considerable alteration in the government of alteration in
Church or State. Church or State: (43) and Consequently,
from the very therefore (18) *all* inventions outset, it was
necessary to resort were set on *foot from the* (15) to every conceivable device*beginning* to work upon (5) for the
purpose of perverting *them,* and (11) corrupt (5) this honest majority into rebellion. *them,* (43) (45) by suggestions
"of the dangers (8) *which* With some, the appeal was
threatened all that was precious addressed to their pa-
triotism. to the subject (19) in their They were warned "of
the liberty and their property, by dangers that threatened
[all *overthrowing* (47 *a*) *or that was precious in]* the liberty
overmastering the law, *and* (47 and property of the subject, *a*) *subjecting* it to *an if the laws were to be made arbi-
trary* (47_a_) *power,* and by subservient to despotism, and
countenancing Popery to the if Popery was to be encour-
aged subversion of the Protestant to the subversion of the
Protestant religion," and then, by religion." infusing ter-
rible apprehensions into some, and so working upon The
fears of others were appealed their fears, (6 *b*) "of (11 *a*)
to. "There was danger," so[21] it being called in question for
was said, "that they might be somewhat they had done,"

---

21. The personality of the tempters and organizers of the conspiracy is
   purposely kept in the background.

by which called to account for something (5) *they* would stand in need of they had done, and they would then (5) *their* protection; and (43) stand in need of the help of those (45) raising the hopes of others, who were now giving them this "that, by *concurring* (47 *a*) timely warning." In others, hopes *with* (5) *them* (5) *they* were excited, and offices, should be sure to obtain offices honours, and preferments were held and honours and any kind of out as the reward of adhesion. preferment." Though there were too Too many were led away by one or many corrupted and misled by these other of these temptations, and several temptations, and (19) indeed some needed no other others (40 *a*) who needed no temptation than their innate other temptations than from the fierceness and barbarity and the fierceness and barbarity *of malice they had contracted against their* (47 *a*) *own natures*, and the Church and the court. But the the malice they had contracted leaders of the conspiracy were not against the Church and against the many. The flock was large and court; (43) yet the number was not submissive, but the shepherds were great *of those in whom the very few. government of the rest* (47 *a*) *was vested*, nor were there many who had the absolute authority (13) to lead, though there were a multitude (13) that was disposed to follow.

(44) (30) Mr. Pym was looked upon Of these, Mr. Pym was thought as the man of greatest experience superior to all the rest in in parliaments, *where he had* parliamentary experience. To this (50) *served very long*, and *was advantage he added habits of always* (50) *a man of business*, business acquired from his (7) being an officer in the continuous service in the Exchequer, (43) and of a good Exchequer. He had also a good reputation generally, (30) though reputation generally; for, though known to be inclined to the known to be inclined to the Puritan party; yet not of those Puritan party, yet he was not so furious resolutions

against the fanatically set against the Church Church as
the other leading men as the other leaders. In this were,
and (44) wholly devoted to respect he resembled the Earl
of the Earl of Bedford, who had Bedford, to whom he was
nothing of that spirit. thoroughly devoted.

(Here follow descriptions of Hampden and Saint John.)

It was generally believed that These three persons,
with the these three persons, with the three peers mentioned before, were other three lords mentioned united in
the closest confidence, before, were of the most intimate
and formed the mainspring of the and entire trust with
each other, party. Such at least was the and made *the en-*
gine which (47 general belief. But it was clear *a) moved* all
the rest; (30) that they also admitted to their yet it was vis-
ible, that (15) unreserved confidence two others, *Nathaniel*
Fiennes, the second son (45) whom I will now of the Lord
Say, and Sir Harry describe,—*Nathaniel Fiennes, Vane, el-*
dest son to the Secretary, second son of Lord Say, and Sir
and Treasurer of the House, were Harry Vane, eldest son of
the received by them with full Secretary, and Treasurer of
the confidence and without reserve. House.

The former, being a man of good Nathaniel Fiennes,
a man of good parts of learning, and after some parts, was
educated at New years spent in New College in College,
Oxford, where his Oxford, (43) of which his father family
claimed and enjoyed some had been formerly fellow, (43)
privileges in virtue of their that family pretending[22] and
kindred to the founder, and enjoying many privileges there,
as where[23] his father had formerly of kin to the founder,

---

22. The relative is retained in the first two cases, because it conveys the
    reason why Fiennes was educated at New College; and in the third
    case, because the increased "antipathy" is regarded as the natural
    consequence of the residence in Calvinistic Geneva.
23. Claiming

(43) (19) been a fellow. He afterwards spent had spent his time abroad in some time in Geneva and in the Geneva and amongst the cantons of cantons of Switzerland, where Switzerland, (30) where he he increased that natural improved his disinclination to the antipathy to the Church which he Church, with which milk he had had imbibed almost with his been nursed. From his travels he mother's milk.[24] By a singular returned through Scotland (52) coincidence, he came home through (which few travellers took in Scotland (not a very common route their way home) at the time when for returning travellers) just (5) *that* rebellion was in bud: when the Scotch rebellion was in (30) (43) (44) and was very little bud. For some time he was scarcely known, except amongst (5) *that* known beyond the narrow and people, *which conversed* (47 a) exclusive circle of his sect, *wholly amongst themselves,* until until at last he appeared in he was now (15) *found in Parliament. Then, indeed, it was Parliament,* (30) (43) (44) when quickly discovered that he was it was quickly discovered that, likely to fulfil even the fond as he was the darling of his hopes of his father and the high father, so (5) *he* was like to promise of many years. make good whatsoever *he* had for many years promised.

The other, Sir H. Vane, was Fiennes' coadjutor, Sir H. Vane, a man of great natural parts[25] was a man of great natural (45) and of very profound ability. Quick in understanding dissimulation, of a quick and impenetrable in dissembling, conception, and of very ready, he could also speak with sharp, and weighty expression. He promptness, point, and weight. His had an (50) unusual aspect, which, singular appearance, though it though it might naturally proceed might naturally proceed from his from his father and mother, parents, who were not noted for neither of which were

---

24. An insinuation of sedition seems intended.
25. This sentence is a preliminary summary of what follows.

beautiful their beauty, yet impressed men persons, yet (19) made men think with the belief that he had in him there was somewhat in him of something extraordinary, an extraordinary: and (52) his whole impression that was confirmed by life made good that imagination. the whole of his life. His Within a very short time after he behaviour at Oxford, where he returned from his studies in studied at Magdalen College, was Magdalen College in Oxford, where, not characterized, in spite of the (43) though he was under the care supervision of a very worthy of a very worthy tutor, he lived tutor, by a severe morality. Soon not with great exactness, (43) he after leaving Oxford he spent some spent some little time in France, little time in France, and more in and more in Geneva, and, (43) Geneva. After returning to after his return into England, England, he conceived an intense (38) contracted a full prejudice hatred not only against the and bitterness against the Church, government of the Church, which both against the form of the was disliked by many, but also government and the Liturgy, (43) against the Liturgy, which was which was generally in great held in great and general reverence, (15 *a*) *even with reverence. many of those who were not friends* to (5) *the other.* In Incurring or seeming to incur, by his giddiness, which then much his giddiness, the displeasure of displeased, or seemed to his father, who at that time, displease, (30) (43) his father, beside strictly conforming to the who still appeared highly Church himself, was very bitter conformable, and exceedingly sharp against Nonconformists, the young against those who were not, Vane left his home for New (5) *he* transported himself into England. New England, (43) a colony within few years before planted by a This colony had been planted a few mixture of all religions,[26] which years before by men of all sorts

---

26. If "which" is used here according to Rule (8), the meaning is, (*a*) "and their differences;" if it is used for "that," the meaning will be, (*b*) "all religions that were of a nature to dispose &c." I believe (*a*) is the meaning; but I have found difference of opinion on the question.

of disposed the professors to dislike religions, and their the government of the Church; who differences disposed them to (30) (43) (44) were qualified by dislike the government of the the king's charter to choose their Church. Now, it happened that their own government and governors, privilege (accorded by the king's under the obligation, "that every charter) of choosing their own man should take the oaths of government and governors was allegiance and supremacy;" (30) subject to this obligation, "that (43) (5) *which* all the first every man should take the oaths of planters did, when they received allegiance and supremacy." These their charter, before they oaths had been taken, not only by transported themselves from hence, all the original planters, on nor was there in many years after receiving their charter, before the least scruple amongst them of leaving England, but also for many complying with those obligations: years afterwards, without exciting so far men were, *in the infancy* the slightest scruple. Indeed, (15) *of their schism*, from scruples against lawful oaths were refusing to take lawful oaths. unknown[27] in the infancy of the (45) He was no sooner landed English schism. But with the there, but his parts made him arrival of Vane all this was quickly taken notice of, (26) and changed. No sooner had he landed very probably his quality, being than his ability, and perhaps to the eldest son of a some extent his position, as eldest Privy-councillor, might give him son of a Privy-councillor, some advantage; *insomuch* (51) recommended him to notice: and at *that,* when the next season came the next election he was chosen for the election of their Governor. magistrates, he was chosen their governor: (30) (45) (43) in which In his new post, his restless and place he had so ill fortune (26) unquiet imagination found (his working and unquiet fancy opportunity for creating and raising and infusing a thousand diffusing a thousand conscientious scruples of conscience, which (5)

---

27. The following words appear to be emphatic, bringing out the difference between the infancy and the development of schism.

scruples that had not been brought *they* had not brought over with over, or ever even heard of, by the them, nor heard of before) (19) colonists. His government proved a that he unsatisfied with failure: and, mutually them and they with him, dissatisfied, (45) governed and he retransported himself governor parted. Vane returned into England; (30) (43) (44) to England, but not till he had having sowed such seed of accomplished his mischievous task, dissension there, as grew up too not till he had sown the seeds of prosperously, and miserably those miserable dissensions which divided the poor colony into afterwards grew only too several factions, and divisions prosperously, till they split the and persecutions of each (15 *a*) wretched colony into distinct, *other*, (30) (43) which still hostile, and mutually persecuting continue *to the great* (54) factions. His handiwork still *prejudice of that plantation:* remains, and it is owing to (15) insomuch as some of (5) *them, him* that some of the colonists, upon the ground of their first on the pretext of liberty of expedition, liberty of conscience, conscience, the original cause of have withdrawn themselves from (5) their emigration, have withdrawn *their* jurisdiction, and obtained themselves from the old colonial other charters from the king, by jurisdiction and have obtained which, (30) (43) in other forms of fresh charters from the king. government, they have enlarged These men have established new their plantations, within new forms of government, unduly limits adjacent to (5) (15 *a*) enlarged their boundaries, and set *the other.*their plantations, up rival settlements on the within new limits adjacent to (5) borders of the original colony. (15 *a*) *the other.*

BURNET

The principal faults in Burnet's style are (*a*) the use of heterogeneous sentences (see 43); (*b*) the want of suspense (see 30); (*c*) the ambiguous use of pronouns (see 5); (*d*) the omission of connecting adverbs and conjunctions, and an excessive use of *and* (see 44); and (*e*) an abruptness in passing from one topic to another (see 45). The correction of these faults necessarily lengthens the altered version.

ORIGINAL VERSION. PARALLEL VERSION

And his maintaining the honour of He also gratified the English the nation in all foreign feeling of self-respect by countries gratified the (1) maintaining the honour of the *vanity which is very natural* nation in all foreign countries. (50) *to Englishmen*; (30) (43) of So jealous was he on this point which he was *so* (15) (17 *a*) that, though he was not a crowned *careful* that, though he was not head, he yet secured for his a crowned head, yet his (40 *a*) ambassadors all the respect that ambassadors had all the respects had been paid to the ambassadors paid them which our (15) *kings'* of our kings. The king, he said, ambassadors ever had: he said (6 received respect simply as the *b*) the dignity of the crown nation's representative head, was upon the account of the and, since the nation was the nation, *of which the king was* same, the same respect should (50) *only the representative be paid to the*[28] nation's head; so, the nation being the ministers. same, he would have the same regards paid to (41) his ministers.

Another[29] instance of (5) *this* The following instance of jealousy pleased *him* much. Blake with the for the national honour pleased fleet *happened* (50) *to be* at him much. When Blake was at Malaga Malaga before he made war upon with his fleet, before his war Spain: (44) *and* some of his with Spain, it happened that some seamen went ashore, *and* met the of his sailors going ashore and Host carried about; (44) *and* not meeting the procession of the only paid no re-

---

28. The meaning is "*his*, and therefore the *nation's*, ministers." There is a kind of antithesis between "the nation" and "the nation's ministers."

29. No instance has yet been mentioned.

spect to it, but Host, not only paid no respect to laughed at
those who did; (43) it, but even laughed at those who (30)
(51) so one of the priests did. Incited by one of the priests
put the people upon resenting this to resent the indignity,
the indignity; *and* they fell upon people fell on the scoffers
and (5) *them and* beat them severely. beat them severely. On
their When they returned to their ship return to the ship the
seamen (5) *they* complained of (5) complained of this ill-usage, *this* usage; and upon that Blake whereupon Blake sent
a messenger sent a trumpet to the viceroy to to the viceroy
to demand the demand the priest who was the priest who
was the instigator of chief (1) *instrument* in that the outrage. The viceroy answered ill-usage. The viceroy answered
that he could not touch him, as he *he* had no authority over
the had no authority over the priests. (15) *priests*, and so
could not To this Blake replied, that he did dispose of him.
Blake upon that not intend to inquire to whom the sent him
word that *he* would not authority belonged, but, if the inquire who had the (1) power to priest were not sent within
three send the priest to him, but if hours, he would burn the
town. The *he* were not sent within three townspeople being
in no condition hours, *he* would burn their town; to resist,
the priest was at once (43) and (5) *they*, being in no sent. On
his arrival, he defended condition to resist *him*, sent himself, alleging the insolence of the priest to *him*, (43) (44) who
the sailors. But the English (50) justified himself upon the
Admiral replied that a complaint petulant behaviour of the
seamen. should have been forwarded to him, and then he
would have punished (44) Blake answered that, if (5) *them*
severely, for none of his *he* had sent a complaint to sailors
should be allowed to *him of it*, *he* would affront the established religion have punished them severely, since of any
place where they touched. *he* would not suffer *his* "But," he
added, "I take it ill men to affront the established that you
should set on your religion of any place at which countrymen to do my work; for I *he* touched; but *he* will have all the

world know that took it ill, that *he* set on the an Englishman
is only to be Spaniards to do *it*; for *he* punished, by an Englishman." Then, would have all the world to know satisfied with having had the that an Englishman was only to
be offender at his mercy, Blake punished by an Englishman;
entertained him civilly and sent and so he treated the priest
him back. civilly, and sent him back, being satisfied that he
had him at his mercy.

Cromwell was much delighted with Cromwell was
much delighted with *this*, and read the Blake's conduct.
Reading the letters in council with great letters in council
with great satisfaction; *and* said he satisfaction, he said, "I
hope I hoped he should make the name of shall make the
name of an an Englishman as great as ever Englishman
as much respected as that of a Roman *had ever was the
name of Roman." been*. The States of Holland Among other
countries the States were in such dread of him that of Holland were in such dread of they took care to give him no
sort Cromwell that they took care to of umbrage; *and* when
give him no sort of umbrage. at any time the king or his
Accordingly, whenever the king or brothers came to see
their sister his brothers came to see the the Princess Royal,
within a Princess Royal their sister, they day or two after,
they used were always warned in a day or two to send a
deputation to let *them* by a deputation that Cromwell had
know that Cromwell had required of required of the States
to give the States that *they* should them no harbourage.
give *them* no harbour.

* * * * * * * * *

Cromwell's favourite alliance was The free kingdom
of Sweden was Sweden.[30] (44) Carolus Gustavus Cromwell's favourite ally; not and he lived in great conjunc-

---

30. The thought that is implied, and should be expressed, by the words,
      is this: "Cromwell's favourite ally was a free country."

tion only under Charles Gustavus, with of counsels. (44) Even Algernon whom he was on most confidential Sydney, (10 *a*) *who* was not terms, but also under Christina. inclined to think or speak well of Both these sovereigns had just kings, commended *him* (5) to me; notions of public liberty; at and said *he* (5) had just least, Algernon Sydney, a man notions of public liberty; (44) certainly not prejudiced in favour (43) *and* added, that Queen of royalty, assured me this was Christina seemed to have *them* true of Gustavus. He also held the likewise. But (44) she was same opinion of Queen Christina; much changed from that, when but, if so, she was much changed I waited on her at Rome; for when I waited on her at Rome; for she complained of us as a factious she then complained of the factious nation, *that did not readily and unruly spirit of our nation.* comply with *the commands* (47 *a*) *of our princes.* (44) All Italy All Italy, no less than trembled at the name of Cromwell, Holland,[31] trembled at the name and seemed under a (1) *panic* as of Cromwell, and dreaded him till long as he lived; (43) his fleet he died. Nor durst the Turks scoured the Mediterranean; and the offend the great (50) Protector Turks durst not offend him; but whose fleet scoured the delivered up Hyde, who kept up the Mediterranean; and they even gave character of an ambassador from up Hyde, who, for keeping up in the king there (23) (43), and was Turkey the character of ambassador brought over and executed for (5) from the king, was brought to *it.* England and executed.

The *putting* the In another instance of severity brother of the king of Portugal's towards foreigners—the execution ambassador to death for murder, of the brother of the Portuguese was (11 *a*) *carrying* justice ambassador for murder—Cromwell very far; (43) since, though in carried

---

31. The remarks about Christina are a digression, and Burnet is now returning to the respect in which Cromwell was held by foreign nations.

justice very far. For, the strictness of the law of though in strictness the law of nations, it is only the nations exempts from foreign ambassador's own person that is jurisdiction the ambassador alone, exempted from (4) *any authority* yet in practice the exemption has (47 *a*) *but his master's that extended to the whole of the sends him*, yet the practice has ambassador's suite. gone in favour of *all that the ambassador owned* (47 *a*) *to Successful abroad, Cromwell was no belong to him*. (41) (44) Cromwell less successful at home in showed his good (11) selecting able and worthy men for*understanding* in nothing more public duties, especially for the than in seeking[32] out capable courts of law. In nothing did he and worthy men for all employments, show more clearly his great but most particularly for the natural insight, and nothing courts of law, (43) (30 *a*) contributed more to his popularity. (10 *a*) which gave a general satisfaction.

BISHOP BUTLER

The principal faults in this style are (*a*) a vague use of pronouns (5), and sometimes (*b*) the use of a phrase, where a word would be enough (47 *a*).

ORIGINAL VERSION. PARALLEL VERSION

Some persons, (15) *upon Some persons avowedly reject all pretence*[33] *of the sufficiency of revelation as*[34] *essentially the light of Nature*, avowedly incredible and necessarily re-

---

32. He not only sought, but sought successfully. That "find" is not necessarily implied by "seek out" seems proved by the use of the word in the Authorized Version, 2 Tim. ii. 17: "He *sought* me *out* very diligently, and *found* me.

33. "To pretend" once meant "to put forward," "maintain."

34. It has been suggested, however, that by "in its very notion incredible," is meant "inconceivable."

ject all revelation as, *in its* fictitious, on the ground that the (47 *a*) *very notion*, light of Nature is in itself incredible, *and what* (47 *a*) sufficient. And assuredly, had the *must be fictitious*. And indeed light of Nature been sufficient in (32) it is certain that no such a sense as to render revelation would have been given, revelation needless or useless, no (32) had the light of Nature been revelation would ever have been sufficient in such a sense as to given. But let any man consider render (5) *one* not[35] wanting, the spiritual darkness that once or useless. But no (15 *b*) man in (41) prevailed in the heathen seriousness and simplicity can world before revelation, and that possibly think *it* (5) *so*, who (41) still prevails in those considers the state of religion in regions that have not yet received the heathen world before the light of revealed truth; above revelation, and *its* (5) present all, let him mark not merely the state in those (11) *places* (8) natural inattention and ignorance *which* have borrowed no light of the masses, but also the from (5) it; particularly (19) the doubtful language held even by a doubtfulness of some of the (12) Socrates on even so vital a greatest men concerning *things of subject as*[36] *the immortality of the utmost* (11) *importance*, as the soul; and then can he in well as the (15 *a*) *natural seriousness and sincerity maintain inattention and ignorance of that the light of Nature is mankind in general*. It is (34) sufficient? impossible to say (12) who would have been able to have reasoned It is of course impossible to deny out that whole system which we that some second[36] Aristotle call natural religion, (30) in its might have reasoned out, in its genuine simplicity, clear of genuine simplicity and without superstition; but there is a touch of superstition, the certainly no ground to affirm whole of that system which we that the generality could.

---

35. "Wanting" is used for modern "wanted."
36. This use of the particular for the general would be out of place in Butler's style, but it adds clearness.

call natural religion. But there (44) If they could, there is is certainly no ground for no sort of probability that affirming that this complicated they would. (44) Admitting there process would have been possible were, they would highly want a for ordinary men. Even if they had standing admonition to remind them had the power, there is no of (5) *it*, and inculcate it upon probability that they would have them. And further still, were (5) had the inclination; and, even if *they* as much *disposed* (47 *a*) we admit the probable inclination, *to attend to* religion as the they would still need some better sort of men (15 *a*) *are*; standing admonition, whereby yet, even upon this supposition, natural religion might be there would be various occasions suggested and inculcated. Still for supernatural instruction and further, even if we suppose these assistance, *and the greatest ordinary men to be as attentive to advantages* (50) *might be religion as men of a better sort, afforded* (15 *a*) *by* (5) yet even then there would be *them*. So that, to say revelation various occasions when is a thing superfluous, *what supernatural instruction and there* (47 *a*) *was no need of*, assistance might be most and *what can be of* (47 *a*) *no beneficially bestowed. service*, is, I think, to talk wildly and at random. Nor would it Therefore, to call revelation be more extravagant to affirm that superfluous, needless, and (40 *a*) *mankind* is so entirely useless, is, in my opinion, to (40 *a*) *at ease* in the present talk wildly and at random. A man state, and (40 *a*) *life so* might as reasonably assert that we completely (40 *a*) *happy*, that are so entirely at ease and so (5) *it* is a contradiction to completely happy in this present suppose (40 *a*) our condition life that our condition cannot capable of *being in any respect* without contradiction be supposed (47 *a*) *better.*—(*Analogy of capable of being in any way Religion*, part ii. chap. 1.) improved.

BREVITY

Sir Archibald Alison

The following extract exhibits examples of tautology and lengthiness. The "implied statement" (50) can often be used as a remedy, but, more often, the best remedy is omission.

ORIGINAL VERSION. PARALLEL VERSION

The Russian empire is (50) *a Russia, with her vast strength and state of* (54) *such* vast boundless resources, is obviously strength and boundless destined to exercise on the course resources, *that* it is of history a great and lasting obviously destined to make a influence. The slowness of her great and lasting impression on progress only renders her human affairs. Its (50) progress durability more probable. The has been slow, but (5) *it*[37] is Russian Empire has not, like the only on that account the more empires of Alexander the Great and likely to be durable. (5) *It* has Napoleon, been raised to sudden not suddenly risen to greatness, greatness by the genius of like the empire of Alexander in individuals or the accidents of ancient (19) (31), or that of fortune, but has been slowly Napoleon in modern, times, from enlarged and firmly consolidated the force of individual genius, or by well-guided ambition and the accidents of (54) casual persevering energy,[38] during a fortune, but has slowly advanced, long succession of ages and (40 *a*) been firmly consolidated (15) *during a succession of ages*, from the combined influence of ambition skilfully directed and energy (15 *a*) *perseveringly applied.*

* * * * * * * * *

---

37. Apparently "it" means, not "progress," but the "Russian empire."
38. Not "energy," but "a long succession of ages," needs to be emphasized.

The extent and fertility of the The extent and fertility of her Russian territory are *such* (54) territory furnish unparalleled *as to* furnish facilities of facilities for the increase of her increase and elements of strength population and power. European *which no nation* (47 *a*) *in the Russia, that is, Russia to the world enjoys.* European west of the Ural Mountains, Russia—that is, Russia to the contains one million two hundred westward of the Ural thousand square geographical Mountains—contains a hundred and miles, or ten times the surface of fifty thousand four hundred square Great Britain and Ireland. marine leagues, or about one million two hundred thousand square geographical miles, being ten times the surface of the British Islands, which contain, including Ireland, one hundred and twenty-two thousand. Great part, This vast territory is intersected no doubt, of this *immense* (54, by no mountain ranges, no arid see below) *territory is covered* deserts; and though much of it is with forests, or (40 *a*) *lies* rendered almost unproductive of so far to the north as to be food either by the denseness of almost unproductive of food; but forests, or by the severity of the no ranges of mountains or arid northern winter, yet almost all, deserts intersect the *vast* (54, except that part which touches see above) *extent,* and almost the Arctic snows, is capable of the whole, excepting that which yielding something for the use touches the Arctic snows, is of man. capable of yielding something for the use of man. The (3) (54) The steppes of the south present *boundless* steppes of the south an inexhaustible pasturage to present (54) *inexhaustible* those nomad tribes whose numerous fields of pasturage, and give and incomparable horsemen form the birth to those nomad tribes, in chief defence of the empire. whose numerous and incomparable horsemen the chief defence of the empire,[39] as of all Oriental states, (15 *a*) *is to be found.*

---

39. There is nothing in the context that requires the words, "as of all Oriental states."

The rich arable lands in the heart The rich arable lands in the of the (54) *empire* produce an interior produce grain enough to (2) *incalculable* quantity of support four times the present grain, capable not only of population of the empire, and yet maintaining four times (5) *its* leave a vast surplus to be present inhabitants, but affording transported by the Dnieper, the a vast surplus for exportation by Volga, and their tributaries, into the Dnieper, the Volga, and their the Euxine or other seas. tributary streams, (30) which *form so many* (54) *natural outlets* into the Euxine or other seas; (44) while the cold and Lastly, the cold bleak plains shivering plains which stretch stretching towards Archangel and towards Archangel and the shores towards the shores of the White of the White Sea are (48) covered Sea, and covered with immense with immense forests of fir and forests of oak and fir, furnish oak, furnishing at once (54)[40] materials for shipbuilding and *inexhaustible* materials for supplies of fuel that will for shipbuilding and supplies of fuel. many generations supersede the (54) *These ample stores* for many necessity of searching for coal. generations will supersede the necessity of searching in the (14 *a*) *bowels* of the earth for *the purposes of* (54) *warmth or manufacture.*

Formidable as the power of Russia Much as we may dread Russia for is from the vast extent of its the vastness of her territory and territory, and the great and of her rapidly increasing numbers, rapidly increasing number *of there is greater cause for fear its* (54) *subjects*, (5) *it* is in the military spirit and the still more (5) *so* from the docility of her people. military spirit and docile disposition *by which they are* (54)[41] *distinguished*. The prevailing (54) *passion* of

40. If they were really "inexhaustible," the "necessity of searching in the bowels of the earth" would be "superseded," not for "many," but for all generations.
41. The words can be implied, and besides they are expressed in the following sentence.

the A burning thirst for conquest is nation is the (54) *love of as prevalent a passion in Russia conquest*, and this (54) *ardent* as democratic ambition in the free (54) *desire*, which (54) *burns states of Western Europe. This as* (54) *fiercely* in them as passion is the unseen spring democratic ambition does in the which, while it retains the free states of Western Europe, is Russians in the strictest the unseen spring[42] which both discipline, unceasingly impels retains them *submissive* (54) their united forces against all *under the standard of their adjoining states. chief* and impels their accumulated forces in ceaseless The national energy, which is as violence over all the adjoining great as the national territory, states. The energies of the rarely wastes itself in disputes people, great as[43] the territory about domestic grievances. For all they inhabit, are rarely wasted in internal evils, how great soever, internal disputes. Domestic the Russians hope to find a grievances, how great soever, are compensation, and more than a (54) overlooked in the thirst for compensation, in the conquest of foreign aggrandizement. (15) In the world. the conquest of the world the people hope to find a compensation, and more than a compensation, (15 *a*) *for all the evils of their interior administration.*

— THE END —

---

42. The metaphor is questionable; for a "spring," *qua* "spring," does not retain at all; and besides, "a passion" ought not to "burn" in one line, and be a "spring" in the next.
43. The meaning appears *not* to be, "great as" (is), *i.e.* "though the territory is great."

Made in the USA
Monee, IL
07 July 2026

56548169R00073